THE GREAT TURNING

The Great Turning

Rennie Davis

2003
Galde Press, Inc.
Lakeville, Minnesota

The Great Turning
© Copyright 2003 by Rennie Davis
All rights reserved.
Printed in the United States of America
No part of this book may be used or reproduced in any
manner whatsoever without written permission from the
publishers except in the case of brief quotations embodied
in critical articles and reviews.

First Edition
First Printing, 2003

Cover design by Gail Carey

Library of Congress Cataloging-in-Publication Data

Davis, Rennie.
  The great turning / Rennie Davis.-- 1st ed.
     p. cm.
  ISBN 1-931942-09-9 (trade pbk.)
  1. Social change. 2. Civilization--Philosophy. 3. Evolution.
4. Philosophy. I. Title.
  HM831.D38 2003
  303.4--dc22
                                    2003018177

Galde Press, Inc.
PO Box 460
Lakeville, Minnesota 55044–0460

the great turning...

Dedicated to

Lia
Maya
Sky

...a new humanity

Revolution

Times change and with them their demands.
In the world cycle there is spring and autumn in
the life of peoples and nations and
these call for social transformations.

Fire in the lake: the image of revolution

Thus the superior man
Sets the calendar in order
And makes the seasons clear.

We master the changes in nature by noting their regularity.
In this way order and clarity appear
in the apparently chaotic changes of the seasons.
We are able to adjust ourselves in advance
To the demands of the different times.

I Ching

Contents

Preface

Inspiration for this book began with the teachings of Sheradon Bryce. In discovering her discourses years ago, I felt drawn to organize a collection of new information into a brief summary. Her work can be more fully accessed at www.riosabeloco.com. Any mistakes in interpreting her material are strictly my own.

As the drumbeat of global intensity registers on every human life, people call for understanding. Conventional explanations no longer seem adequate. This little book is a big-picture journey into today's confusing volatility, including weather patterns, road rage, emotional overload, sleep deprivation, bizarre dreams, and a continuous world crisis that seems to leap from one region to the next.

The Great Turning views the modern juncture from a new perspective. Should you find excitement here, more excitement is coming as an age of discovery enters our world.

I have friends who are scientists. My three brothers and my sister live normal, practical lives. While I feel excitement that this book finds its way to print, its unsubstantiated theories are bound to challenge old friends and practical family members. Perhaps a hundred years from now, there may be smiles that hidden mysteries could be seen through veils. Today, however, any new theory about previously veiled subjects—outside the empirical evidence known to science—raises eyebrows, as it should.

I mean no disrespect to any science or sacred belief with this account of reality. Should something you discover in these pages fit, or work for you, it belongs to you. If the information encounters resistance as a result of previous understandings in science, religion, culture or philosophy, I mean no offense.

I appreciate the deep challenge of presenting this extraordinary information.

When I propose the existence of a mechanism, or switch, that clicks off and then back on again in a rare but natural occurrence in the universe, I understand no science can know this mechanism to exist and no evidence is likely to validate this on/off/on universal moment, at least not before it is over. Having no intent to solicit anyone's leap of faith, I invite the reader to consider another approach. You can question this information by employing new methods of gathering data inherent in yourself.

You have fourteen senses, not five. When you give yourself permission to receive information using your radar, sonar, or the other senses biologists have yet to uncover, you may astound yourself. Extraordinary information comes to you in response to your desire to know. Your human body is a data-gathering wonder. Transferring what you already know unconsciously to the conscious level is also possible. Learning to employ your data sensing abilities, you may discover a way to draw your own road map for the time of the Great Turning.

Knowing there are veils about our human origin, the physics of atomic structure, and the great cycles of evolution, it may seem impossible to evaluate this text. I respect that viewpoint but disagree. It is feasible to know the time in which you live. You can sense and comprehend the central event of this generation.

When the silent, invisible hand of evolution comes dramatically to the forefront to touch every life on earth, those who see evolution at work will celebrate the time of the Great Turning.

Resisting in-coming events with judgment and blame, a river of hell appears. Allowing the Great Turning to touch you like an intimate friend, you access an unconditional material called life in an experience that causes body changes. With body changes, evidence of evolution at work is discovered.

How can you relax into non-judgment when all around you everyone is stressed and judgmental? How can you disconnect from the fearful thoughts of others? This book encourages you to ask questions and give yourself permission to believe authentic answers await you. When you have a question, the answer has arrived wanting to show itself. Questions mean answers are already known inside.

You live in a time when evidence for the Great Turning surrounds you, its profound meaning accessible when you ask. You can bring the information forward within yourself. Nothing is hidden. You hear the coming time from your own deep listening.

Acknowledgments

Writing this book was a solitary act but helping hands showed up all around me. These are the people whose gift of support made possible the adventure you are about to engage. My appreciation goes to Valerie Albicker, Sheradon Bryce, Gail Carey, Kat Cathey, Rhonda Day, Jami Fachinello, Mark Fledderjohn, Judith Green, Dave Kolko, Sabe Loco, Makasha, Maureen McBride, Galde Press, Moki Skye, Jaz Taylor, Bob Schmutz, Linda Stuhlman and Teresa Wenz.

Thank you for your kindness.

Call to Humanity

A sweeping change envelops the world, driven by events not fully comprehended. Traditional frameworks once relied upon to understand society no longer seem adequate. Psychic breakups ending in the murder of mothers and children, commercial airliners flying into twin towers, suicide bombers exploding in crowded places, the fiery ravage of forests started by government employees hired to protect them—in the bombardment of such daily news the human will to act contrary to its own self interest challenges our capacity to understand or cope.

As nations engage in a new war on terrorism, polarization of ancient moral wars pulls governments and cultures into "no-option" stand offs. With a proliferation of no-options, the polarization intensifies, spreading like an epidemic with no name. It is not just global conflicts intensifying—dreams are intensifying too. Sleep deprivation is intensifying. The weather is intensifying. Human disrespect is intensifying. Even calls for Jihad and Armageddon are intensifying, as no-option beliefs take hold in mainstream, normal people.

Polarization may describe the modern condition, but what is its cause? We may recognize that humanity has come to the riverbank, but why?

1

People admit the strangeness in their growing sense of connection among the world's troubling events. The suspicion grows nevertheless that a connection is operating in rain forest devastation, water contaminations, child kidnappings, killer viruses, food insecurity, ethnic cleansing, weapons of mass destruction, worldwide terrorism, United Nation breakdowns, and the fires, winds, rains, volcanoes, tornadoes, and global warming that define the new century. To suggest connections among previously unrelated events may trouble the rational scientist, but when satisfactory answers cannot be found in science, sociology, psychology, or history, the need to understand what threatens humanity becomes a new global agenda.

A contrary-to-life belief system has staked its claim in the human condition. When one's beliefs cause behavior contrary to one's own evolutionary self-interest, tiny annoyances and everyday disappointments trigger deadly showdowns. Frustration turns to intense irritability as quickly as irritability explodes into road rage. As millions of people wonder if suicide bombings are their only option, others ask if the human psyche is turning on itself like a disordered immune system, consuming the body that houses it. While the cause of contrary behavior may elude us, its effect marches on, gathering into a worldwide tension and swelling towards a thunderous storm.

Triumph over "Contrary" has been achieved in every age and culture. A person unlocks the chains of their own negativity to walk free of Contrary. Overcoming the resistance of family, friends, and neighbors, such people become known as "saints" to future generations, who honor them in diverse religions and stories. They created their own sacred reality, without blaming or judging others, and their example inspires the world.

Any human being in any time or place has the right and capacity to create their own reality. In this simple understanding, the modern condition of Contrary could become the genesis for a new human being.

In earlier times when people lived in tribes and hunted and gathered food, starvation resulted when food became scarce. Then came the concept of farming, as hunters learned to cultivate the soil, plant seeds, and experience the increased control over famine made possible by the vision of agriculture. In learning to feed ourselves, we evolved from the scarcity of hunting and gathering. In the same fashion, a new vision can lead humanity to evolve again, changing the condition of Contrary into something new.

Contrary believes "if one thing doesn't get me, something else will." When we believe the negative events affecting our lives originate from outside ourselves, our distrusting beliefs find evidence to confirm themselves. In this way, the modern condition of Contrary evolved.

Contrary grows naturally from the conscious and unconscious beliefs we hold about ourselves: Victim. Unworthiness. Hate. A single thought, unnoticed by nearly all people, is the mother of experience.

In the past, when people freed themselves from Contrary, a non-judging trust for life was enthusiastically embraced by a person able to believe that "everything that happens to me is going to be more magnificent than anything I could have imagined." Deeply held, such vision caused extraordinary experiences. Blaming no one for misfortune, they realized "all my chains are forged by thought." In the decision to trust and the intention to love, beauty entered their lives. Stories from every time and culture describe the transforming experiences of people who understood such principles.

The understanding of non-judgment can be daunting or seem wrong to those who work hard to make the world a better place. Is it not inappropriate to show respect for a person who plunders the environment or obstructs the democratic will? Bad people must be punished. When someone is wrong, they are demonized for good reason. In previous generations, the person who had no judgment towards others was considered a fool. Indeed, a person able to see the deep purpose in all people, regardless of their "wrong-doings" has been the fool in every age. Nevertheless, in the lives of Lao Tse, Buddha, Jesus, Athanasium of Egypt, Father of Ethiopia, Benedict the

Moor, Our Lady of the Angels, St. John, Rumi, the Buddhist saint Shantideva, Mahatma Gandhi, Mother Teresa, Martin Luther King, Jr., the Dalai Lama, and many others, we witness the fool inspiring the world with a simple understanding. The bonds of Contrary are easily broken in the choice to respect and love life.

How do we comprehend the emotional pull and new intensity of Contrary? People today, touching into Contrary, quickly find themselves running through a river of hell. As governments and terrorists, polluters and earth saviors, conservatives and liberals, Palestinians and Israelis, Muslims and Christians, and husbands and wives engage in no-option side-taking, polarization suddenly becomes the trap itself. Emotional overload sets in, whether one is on the "good side" or "bad side." Is there a deeper cause working? Is humanity at a crossroads?

The Call To Humanity understands our time as a crossroads in human evolution. Not a call to take sides or fix the condition of Contrary with more polarization, it is an invitation to walk out of human negativity altogether and experience the life that results when the need to blame or condemn others has perished. In replacing the choice to take sides with a curiosity for all sides, global family emerges, embracing humanity unconditionally, not by dividing or polarizing but by knowing, accepting, and becoming every person engaged. It is our love for humanity that inspires people to consider their own sacred purpose. It is our creativity, flowing naturally out of acceptance, that generates new possibilities on earth.

An example of the new creativity may be found in technologies now arriving. From unexpected quarters, breakthrough discoveries stimulate possibilities where deadlock has set in. One day we may smile, realizing that it was our own need to move out of Contrary that drew these technologies to us in the first place.

Not the small incremental technological advancements common to the large corporate enterprise, breakthrough discoveries are coming—as world-changing as Edison's light bulb or Tesla's alternating current. While rare events in history, breakthrough technologies may encourage new dreams where no-option beliefs now prevail. In the industries of housing, water, energy, food, health, clean air, waste management, and environmental restoration, answers await in these extraordinary discoveries.

Often the achievement of a single individual, working alone and outside of mainstream institutions, these inventors may sense "spirit" behind their work. Like Mozart, Einstein, and Tesla in that respect, the inventors of modern breakthroughs often claim their "genius" derives from an invisible hand.

Breakthrough technologies are in basements and

garages and home laboratories, waiting to connect to entrepreneurs able to orchestrate large-scale commercial or humanitarian undertakings. While most are not commercially available now, they may become available as we invite and see them as components of a new dream for humanity.

It is not just new vision technologies that are possible. Creative people are appearing as well, with local and global solutions in hand. Calling them into service are forgotten villages, teeming cities, starving children, and failing ecosystems where options and hope have virtually expired. Motivated by a love for humanity, their passion to serve represents a new respect entering the world.

Every nation creates a culture holding its values and customs. The nation that nourishes respect as its culture unlocks an innate human potential able to send out an invisible influence. The power of respect to shape the world comes from its unconditional nature, an influence that quickly dissipates when turned on and off, giving respect to some while denying it to others. Where people offer respect unconditionally, a unique creativity is unleashed.

In a nation of respect, citizens embrace respect as their own deep purpose. Technologies are developed for their respect of nature and people. Businesses are created that understand the value of constantly renewing the qualities from which respect grows, and creating enterprises that are fertile soil for people to contribute without ulterior designs.

To sustain a culture of respect—perhaps the ultimate challenge of humanity—a daily renewal of character is required. Blaming or judging others may be common to the modern time but respect in a new humanity will never make those who disrespect wrong. Respect is simply the natural preference when leaving the condition of Contrary.

Respect engages others with innocence and curiosity. Where curiosity has replaced the need to make others wrong, the mind becomes natural. Where the mind is natural and unconditional, a person embraces life with an instinctive sureness. Infusing life into every activity, divergent aims fall away, fellowship appears in the open and people can accomplish the task that is great.

Can one person's triumph over Contrary in an earlier time germinate the seeds of evolution in a new person today? When the answer is yes, one person can be two and two may be four and four can be millions. Indeed, one person, holding unconditional respect as a new standard on earth, can midwife the birth of a new humanity.

The Phoenix was a mythological bird able to consume itself in flame. Nothing remained but an ashen seed from which the Phoenix would rise again in a new beginning.

In today's world, many people feel their life is melting down. From today's fiery consumption, a person can birth again, their passion unbridled, their life touching the creativity that flows naturally from the unconditional mind.

In a time of possibilities, the dream of humanity emerges from our choice. To chose Contrary or to embrace life is the choice before us. Choosing life in the time of Contrary, the dream of humanity cannot perish. Embracing humanity in its time of evolution, a new humanity rises like the Phoenix, secure in the proposition that life shall be the new social agreement, and unconditional respect the covenant for a new human being on earth.

To Paint a Picture

Humanity is a grand idea. To dream the most magnificent entity in existence out of nothing at all is imagination on a grand scale. The story of human evolution was born of an incomprehensible imagination.

The Great Turning is not an argument to annoy the great traditions, religions, philosophies or scientific cosmologies. Critics of this understanding will encounter no defense. This is new information for those who are drawn to consider the grand vision of humanity and the invisible cycles and forces underlying an historic transition.

To understand this time, we go backwards to our origin and then to the future that pulls us towards a vision of divine human. The Great Turning sees the coming years of transition in the context of evolution and interprets current events from a perspective of large cycles that occur naturally in this world.

Great shifts in understanding are slow to take hold. When new understanding is set forth, many prefer to hold tightly to familiar perceptions. The human psyche is comfortable with how it understands. There is nothing inappropriate when one's perception of reality helps one navigate through an extraordinary time of change.

The person who holds tightly to a familiar story in the time of the Great Turning makes an appropriate decision. Staying steady with existing beliefs, he or she supports the stability of the psyche at a time when global psychic change becomes a defining event.

However, for those who ask for an authentic framework to understand this time of change—for those who want nothing held back—an adventure of discovery awaits. The origin of our universe, the blueprint of humanity, understanding deity, great cycles of evolution—previously veiled subjects can be uncovered by this generation like no other before it.

The Great Turning may serve as a forerunner to knowledge that is your birthright—a tiny path of breadcrumbs in the form of clues and navigational tools to assist your journey into understanding the coming juncture of evolution. May it support your inquiry into the design of this world and the time in which you live.

When you ask deeply and sincerely, the age of discovery appears.

The Great Turning was foretold by shamans, seers and saints in virtually every generation. But there were veils hiding the coming events, even from those with the gift of sight. You, however, are the generation that will experience this time. You are the fruit of the human tree, the first generation able to step through veils to sense and prepare for the time that is coming.

Events are occurring for which there is no historical framework. Changes are taking place for which no conventional explanation seems satisfactory. Many people feel an acceleration of anxiety building within them, taking them in a direction for which they have no explanation. In the thoughts of humanity, consensus seems to be unraveling, not just in far-away lands but in neighborhoods nearby. Intensification of judgment, disrespect towards others, polarization and blame—symptoms describing the modern human condition are easily listed but beg the deeper question: Why?

The framework of consciousness upon which humanity has secured its global consensus is becoming destabilized.

On September 11, 2001, hundreds of millions of people shifted into a new understanding as twin towers in New York city collapsed in an attack of hate. Long before September 11, however, observant people noticed an emotional intensity building in the human race. People wondered, is disrespect the new public standard? Is there an increase in road rage, or are recent road rage reports simply the result of better journalism? Why do historical prejudices seem to jump out of the grave, plunging modern nations into ancient nightmares? Are weather anomalies a permanent, new reality on earth? Are deadly new viruses increasing? With no particular evidence to cross-link such diverse, troubling events, people nevertheless wonder, is there a deep river beneath the surface of our lives changing our world? Such questions rarely enter our public forums to be discussed, but privately, we have questions. We don't know what to think.

The New York Times recently had the courage to probe today's new weather patterns—angry volcanoes, earthquakes, swollen flood plains, intense fires and other weather anomalies—by asking religious leaders to interpret the spiritual message of the weather. The interview format allowed a leading newspaper to suggest that something mysterious and inexplicable might be at work in our modern weather conditions without losing credibility. Because science and institutions don't know the long-range outlook for the earth's weather, newspaper audiences have questions that no respectable journalist feels comfortable to probe.

Readers have questions about more than just the weather. Why are ex-employees returning to their offices in record numbers to kill and be killed? Why the acceleration of senseless murders by teenagers? Why are millions of people quick to react to the slightest perception of something wrong, even when nothing is wrong? Strong, confident people are emotionally exploding over tiny annoyances and no one can say why.

Perhaps newspapers and governments should conduct public surveys to measure the deep river of psychosis silently swelling in the human community. Scientific research might discover a high percentage of humanity now experiencing new pressures and headaches in the brain, and unfamiliar electrical stimulations in the nervous system. Large numbers of people might report new body pains or intense "energies," especially at night, setting off acidic conditions in their stomachs or anxiety attacks for no apparent reason. Women, including those who never before entertained the validity of horoscopes, wonder if their new roller-coaster emotional state has something to do with planetary conjunctions. Men ask why they possess the symptoms of PMS.

Surveys of psychiatrists and MDs might discover an increase in patient demands for medications to sedate the body and mind from depression, fear, or the instability of psychotic episodes. Psychologists suspect that the dream-state of their patients is changing and sleep deprivation is on the rise. People on summer beaches ask close friends if sleep is becoming a new paranormal phenomenon, or "is it just me?"

No conventional scientific perspective explains the events now unfolding in the world. Forces are at work whose origin is not familiar. Conventional explanations don't hold up. To use the standard categories of psychology, sociology, economics, politics, war, disease, conspiracies, or even astrology is to describe symptoms rather than causes. Unexplained events now pushing into people's lives seem to have no precedents.

As events accelerate and pull us into an unknown future, there is only conjecture to interrupt the unsettling anxiety advancing through the general population. Humanity faces a situation like that of Christopher Columbus, who sailed with no map into uncharted waters, and whose crew wondered if their three ships were about to fall off the edge of the earth. "Sailing the edge" may describe the modern experience, but such descriptions do not satisfy our questions.

Some people believe that humanity has traditions or myths, depicting an earlier time where people experienced this current cycle, the time of the Great Turning. Records from geology or history about a previous Great Turning are slim, and evidence of earlier global shifts are easily challenged by scientists, making people doubt that any prior cycle or repeating historical patterns can be found or sensed, even by those with the gift of clairvoyance.

Nevertheless, the Great Turning seems "known" to people, even when such knowledge is elusive or buried in the unconscious mind. Can conscious understandings about what is happening in our world be discovered? Can anyone authentically know the time in which we live?

To paint a picture of what is coming into humanity may trigger unconscious knowledge and bring it to the conscious surface. However, such a picture may also portray an unfamiliar, alien landscape seeded with "concept bombs." An accurate portrayal of our time may be difficult for the mind to accept. The picture of one reality completing and a new reality coming in is deeply unsettling. Depictions of the Great Turning put pressure on the human psyche. Pressure on the psyche is what we are seeing in today's psychotic episodes.

It is easy to accept scientific evidence that plants and animals evolve. It is not so easy to believe that our own bodies evolve, or that the change now occurring in the world is the result of some precursor of change set to occur in our own atomic structure, DNA, nervous system and physical body.

Humanity has entered an environment for which the brain has no reference. In this new environment, the psyche may either tighten down and fracture, or release and expand into a new awareness.

Everyone is experiencing the deep choices of the time: letting go to invisible life forces now entering this world (an experience that takes you into an ecstatic and expansive state) or tightening down and resisting the in-coming change. Depending on one's choices, you meet people who are open and excited by the new possibilities, and you find those who say "don't bother me" in response to information about the Great Turning.

If you are a person who desires authentic understanding, then understanding is your way to prepare the psyche for what is coming. You have been searching for information. If you are a person who goes to the kitchen to make a sandwich when the living room discussion turns to the subject of the Great Turning, you are probably comfortable with your sense of reality. You know your views will take you through the years of transition. "Sandwich-makers" are choosing to experience the Great Turning without forcing the psyche out of its established understandings. They will get through this period by finding stability in what is familiar. Pressure on them from those who "know what is happening" can be inappropriate.

For those who seek authentic perspectives about the Great Turning, there is no accepted science, geology, or history on which to rely. Challenging as that statement may seem, the possibility of discovering authentic insight into the singular event of this time is nevertheless before you. Even the hope of such discovery should be inspiring. The inspiration comes in part from the incomprehensible height from which any authentic framework must begin, a place where the grandness and magnificence of the human journey can be sensed. Like holding a great telescope that allows you to look upon yourself at the origin of the universe and then see yourself again as the universe completes, the present moment is dazzling to behold.

If you are a seeker of understanding, my advice is to acquire a broad vantage point from which you can watch the in-coming reality appear while the world around you completes and separates out. Your respectful way of seeing will let you ride through any rough spots magically and gracefully. You are okay in whatever you encounter, even "horrific" events, when you hold people in respect. You live in a time like no other. You journey towards a new humanity. Your journey has begun.

Evolution's Blueprint

Our story of humanity starts with an original thought: the concept of self-awareness emerging and evolving inside mass and matter. No physical evidence or science for our story is known. But neither are you without capacity to evaluate this information or discover for yourself what is authentic and what is not.

You are invited to uncover your own abilities to know the hidden and walk through veils. An age of discovery awaits you.

What humanity calls creation—the physical universe—is a new kid on the block. If you could see through the eyes of evolution, you would know that a developed, non-physical universe with diverse, self-aware intelligences existed before our physical creation. Physicality was designed by non-physical intelligences. From their creative thought, our physical universe emerged.

Creation has a blueprint containing the original thought from which the physical universe arose.

Among the components in this blueprint, the design includes the rare gift of omnipresence. Humanity may or may not incorporate this particular feature (at the moment it appears we will not), but omnipresence is an awareness that understands it exists in everything. It is aware of itself in all realities simultaneously. Omnipresence is among a long list of extraordinary possibilities we may one day possess, all of them set forth in evolution's blueprint.

You can touch and know the blueprint of evolution with your mind.

To support the cause of evolution's blueprint, the human body was designed with fourteen senses that allow you to gather information from the furthest reaches of existence. You also have a mind with an unlimited capacity to know. In addition, there is a "small, still voice" in your awareness that serves as a spiritual instinct. You have another instinct or "small, still voice" placed in the biological system—a different instinct coming from the body and not your awareness. The physical equipment that your awareness occupies provides you with unique abilities to gather and store data.

For example, coming out of the skin of your body, you have a mechanism that sends out airborne hormones or pheromones in response to a question or focus. Your circuitry system activates and connects when you think of something. With your mind in focus, you connect to information or archives located in creation. Your body's ability to connect to virtually anything using its high speed, fiber optic-like circuitry is one of numerous mechanisms you possess that allow you to think of an object, person or concept, physically connect to it, access its data, and retrieve the information it holds. You do this now but at an unconscious level.

Using circuitry, you can connect to your original design—the blueprint of evolution, the original thought that describes your future.

We can laugh at this bizarre idea or declare it "impossible," but evolution's blueprint is located in the physical universe. If it exists in physicality, you can find it. You have the equipment at the present time to make your own conclusions about its existence. Finding the blueprint, you can read your future when you are ready.

A strange idea, of course, the blueprint was hidden in every previous generation. Now the veils surrounding it are gone.

The blueprint is the original concept for the evolution of physicality. Each stage of evolution is marked and described by it, including the time of the Great Turning. To read the blueprint is to understand your origin. To touch the blueprint is to see the future of divine human.

How can the body access and know the design of evolution?

The sky is so vast that human imagination has rarely felt an impulse to consider a place beyond the borders of the physical universe. When I was younger, I tended to believe there were no borders—that the universe was seamless and infinite. Many believe the intelligence that created the universe is infinite. Imagining a place beyond the universe is difficult for the human psyche. But to comprehend the concept of a blueprint inside the physical universe, we look first to a place outside the universe.

What we see in the sky on a clear night is not a natural universe but an engineered, holographic space. Our universe is finite, not infinite. The space we occupy has a large stop sign just before a containment wall. You can't go beyond the containment that holds the physical universe.

Physicality is a project of evolution taking place inside a containment, encompassing all the galaxies we see and many we don't see. The shape of the containment is that of a rectangle.

The universe outside the containment protects itself from "contaminants" of thought inside the containment. "Nothing" outside can enter the containment and nothing inside can leave it.

Physicality is a project in which awareness evolves through stages. One day we realize our blueprint and birth out of the containment into a natural universe. In that future time, thoughts of separation, unworthiness, and hate will have ended. Our awareness will be sufficiently mature that our thoughts will no longer be lethal to others outside.

Humanity's destiny is a journey to wonders outside the containment. Beyond the physical universe, wonders await.

Remember the question, which came first, the chicken or the egg? For a creator of universes, the chicken comes first. To create awareness in an engineered space, you first design the end result. The prototype "divine human" intended to be the outcome of physicality was the original idea or blueprint—the chicken placed inside the containment as a force pulling evolution towards it. Humanity is the egg that came after the chicken.

In the early stages of an entity project (such as the physical universe), there may be tweaking and modifications of the prototype chicken, but soon the chicken is given the choice to evolve any way it chooses. The day a chicken is given custody over its own egg is the day the chicken has the ability to evolve, make its own decisions, and add to or change its own DNA. On that day, changes created by the chicken go into the egg as new DNA and those changes direct its evolution as eggs hatch in a progression of chicks. In this oversimplified but essentially accurate analogy, we discover a profound concept about ourselves: we create our Self by what we believe our Self to be. We control our own DNA. Evolution is self-selecting.

The blueprint placed inside this containment is a living entity created to serve the entire development of physicality from beginning to end. Its origin is an intelligence that volunteered to contribute a part of itself to "morph" into the end product, or blueprint of physicality. The part that was shaped into the blueprint was placed in our engineered space as the force of our future, pulling our awareness and biological system over eons and eons towards the original thought of physicality. We become our blueprint when we let go to spirit and allow ourselves to be pulled by the flow of life.

We could say the blueprint is our destiny except for the fact that we also have custody over our own DNA to evolve any way we want. The law of free will and the destiny of evolution operate side by side, and each person gets to choose their evolutionary direction. Where there is free will, you may choose to evolve towards your blueprint or move in an altogether different direction.

The human race has chosen to move away from the blueprint, following social consciousness rather than its original thought.

Having lost connection to the blueprint, human beings in the present time suddenly feel troubled and anxious, knowing at deep levels that they lack the coordinates and road map to navigate the unknowns of the Great Turning described by the blueprint.

Ask and listen deeply to your body. Ask if this is true. Does the body plead for you to access the blueprint in order to evolve? See if you sense yes or no. Should you feel yes inside, you may reconnect to the blueprint. You can respond affirmatively to your body's call.

The blueprint is accessed through the feet, by opening and connecting your feet to a rhythm or cadence generated by the earth. More understanding is available about the rhythm of the earth in the chapter entitled "Campaign for the Earth."

The blueprint is also accessed through the female cervix as a frequency in a heightened stage of sexuality, registering in the body as an ecstatic, semi-conscious state of delirium. The male is a more recent species than the female and cannot access the blueprint in this manner, but males can receive the blueprint through circuitry when picked up from a female partner.

The concept of a blueprint may seem stranger than fiction. To entities outside the containment, physicality seems stranger than fiction.

Imagine that you are involved in a post-graduate biology study. At the end of the course you get a final assignment. You are asked to create a living being or entity inside a rock. You must animate the rock so that it dances around you as it talks to you. Placing awareness inside mass and matter is that strange. A radical idea never considered before the event of physicality, what we take for granted—awareness inside an organic medium evolving in a physical universe—is extraordinary to anyone who came before physicality. Nevertheless, our strange design is valued by non-physical entities. We possess future abilities no one else can claim. The human body that hosts our awareness is a new medium unlike anything that went before. For example, our ability to retrieve and store data is like no previous arrangement.

How can the body collect and store data?

It is possible to take all of the intelligence, data, and information of this universe and compress it into a tiny dot. At the present time, your body holds billions and billions of such compressed knowledge modules or "virals." You are a hardware/software intelligence system able to operate virtually every reality in existence. As your awareness evolves, you will develop the ability to source life material inside your Self. At the present time, that ability does not exist. No self-aware entity can do that. You are a new hybrid species consisting of self, creator, and source. Your body can also morph or shape-shift into any reality imaged by your awareness. You possess a self-aware instrument in which anything you imagine instantly manifests. You also have a psyche, one of the rare developments in evolution. One day, you will create worlds and universes from the physics of thought-done. All of this and more is described in your blueprint.

Should you birth out of the containment into the natural universe, you would be seen by the universal family as the new marvel of creation.

Emerging from billions of years, surviving against all expectations, the current assessment of this project has shifted. Where once we were viewed with skepticism or opposition, today the assessment from outside the containment is one of excitement and hope. Out of the extraordinary possibility that a human being, any human being, might birth out of the containment in the time of the Great Turning, intelligent entities focus on this place like no other time, offering to assist any person who asks. The information in this book is one result.

The potential for something extraordinary to occur in you in the time of the Great Turning draws omnipresent entities outside the containment to support you should you wish to move to the fast track of evolution.

Humanity is a vision that began with a "useless" material—left-over slough-off that remains when an entity moves. Now, billions of years after the discovery that slough-off was an extraordinary genesis medium for a new awareness, the new kid on the block is in a position to return to the natural universe, not as slough-off, but as the new "mass and matter entity" having memory, sensory perception, sourcing abilities, and other features never previously known.

No human being ever realized the blueprint. No prior story or tradition suggests the existence of a blueprint. Our religious traditions and historical cosmologies, including the Christ story, Buddha story, Mohammed story, Lao Tsu, Krishna, Hopi, Mayan, and shaman stories, as well as all the other cosmologies that inspired our cultures' spirituality, never set forth evolution's blueprint. A concept previously veiled, the blueprint points to a future when divine "human" leaves physicality for a place outside the containment in an evolutionary advance in the realms of unlimited beings.

I use the word "physicality" to mean this universe. Physicality is everything within the containment. Physicality includes the factories, automobiles, houses, rain forests, oceans, mountains, and other concrete stuff of our world. But physicality also means all our thoughts and beliefs about God, spirit, and heaven. Physicality incorporates the "dead zone," angels and spirits, and all the other "non-physical" entities of our universe. Our loved ones who went to heaven are inside physicality. Great spirits who say their channeled words speak to us from star systems, inner orders or angelic realms are in physicality. Ascended masters who "watch over humanity from other dimensions" are in physicality. Christ, who ascended to heaven to sit at the right hand of God, remains in physicality. No one who ever existed in physicality has ever left physicality.

Once upon a time, the creators of physicality gathered around to decide on a new creative project. To take slough-off, considered as having no value or purpose, and engineer an entity-source-self hybrid species—such was the original thought. Someone volunteered to be the cosmic clay and allow a portion of their Self to be shaped into the end "chicken"—the prototype or blueprint for physicality. Placed inside the containment, the prototype was a force drawing any awareness that might emerge towards its design.

Once the blueprint was set into the engineered space, it became the chicken with a rope. The chicken could pull the egg into the chick, and the chick into the pullet, until one day the pullet became the fully matured chicken able to leave the hen house.

In high school, I was the Eastern United States chicken judging champion. I helped my Dad raise the critters in fairly large numbers. I held the attitude that chickens were not that bright. I use to tell a joke that starting by asking, "How does a chicken cross the road?" Today, I would answer that it doesn't matter—the chicken can zigzag, go slow, fast, forward, backward, anyway it chooses. Free will is the law of the road. But the law of free will has been joined in this reality to a tractor beam that gently works to pull the chicken to its destination.

The journey of evolution is a journey of free will. You get to the blueprint whatever way you choose. The journey of evolution is also one of destiny. The force of the future turns every path you choose into the perfect path. You are always in perfection. In the mystery of the blueprint, you can't make a wrong turn in your journey of evolution.

Deity

Humanity holds honored stories about deity—stories that inspired the human spirit in every generation. We have stories about unconditional gods and accounts of judgmental, punishing gods. From masculine gods to feminine gods, gods who live outside to gods who live within, the human understanding of deity ranges widely. Some ages believed there was one God. Other times claimed multiple gods serving many purposes. Messengers of God were pathways to God. Channeled communications from God as well as guidance from angels and ascended masters provided prophecies about future times, including the time of the Great Turning. Through our long march of history, the human concept of deity has been a developing one, suggesting future understandings about deity may continue to evolve as well.

The story of deity I present here springs from a love and appreciation for all faiths, beliefs and revelations about our human origin.

A person's faith about God may be tightly held. If you are someone who strongly holds a religious view, I invite you to consider this discussion as backdrop to our central question. Has evolution reached a crossroads? Should

33

you find this description of deity troubling, you are not wrong and no argument is intended.

Different from other historical accounts, this perspective of deity is the result of new information, from places where "friends of humanity" seem to exist. Appearing in the time of the Great Turning, they offer perspectives about our origin, the construction of the universe, and current events. After years of dialogue and observing their intelligence in "virtual laboratories" (where lab results bring new meaning to the word "science"), I call them friends. Their deep level of respect inspires me. Having friends who don't live on earth may seem appropriate to me but can be incomprehensible to anyone engaging these ideas for the first time. Nevertheless, this new account of deity is not a cause to put down your book. Should human concepts of God continue to evolve as they have in the past, perhaps this information one day may find a place in human understanding. If the description of deity expressed here is different than your own, you need not suspend your own viewpoint to hear this one.

What is deity? Is there an origin to deity? Is deity one or many? Did anything exist before deity?

In this new story, before creation existed, there was the "No Thing." For reasons not understood, creation began when movement occurred in the No Thing. Like a weight falling through space, movement in the No

Thing caused something to occur. Something emerged from No Thing in a movement that became "the beginning." Because it is known there was a beginning, it is speculated the natural universe may also once have ended.

In the beginning, self-aware entities and a material, brimming with life but having no self-awareness, emerged. Through eons of evolution, creation today still consists of these two types: (1) self-aware entities, each distinguishable and unique and (2) an unformatted material having no awareness of itself or others but serving as the source of life.

Both self-aware entities and "source" material are deity. Source expands and stops, expands and stops, expands and stops forever. Everything else in creation expands and contracts, expands and contracts. Everything in creation "breathes" except source.

Should Source be called God? Although Source has no awareness of itself and has never created anything from its own awareness, perhaps source is God. With more than one source in the universe, however, the idea of one God could not apply to source.

On the other hand, an entity that is aware of itself in everything and creates with thought through instantaneous manifestation of thought might be called God. Self-aware entities are numerous and possess a diverse range of abilities. Many create by thought. Others create by dreaming. Some entities are omnipresent. Other entities are not. What is God—source or these omnipresent entities that create with thought? What about entities that create by dreaming? What should they be called?

Long ago, I decided to leave it to others to decide what to call God.

Self-aware entities see deity in everything. Nothing exists that is not deity. To them, human understandings about deity put a cap on our evolution into the awareness of deity. What is the awareness of deity? Respect for all, no hierarchy whatsoever and seeing oneself in everything such that a thought of separation never occurs—that is the awareness of deity.

Our world was the result of deity. One entity in particular is credited with the original idea of physicality—serving, so to speak, as "project manager" for the development of physicality. The project manager for our physical universe is an entity that creates by vivid, lucid dreaming.

We know human beings have a dreaming capacity. We are dreamers, but what does dreaming do?

Dreaming is a rare ability that not every entity possesses. The Dreaming unit that stands at the center of our universe goes to sleep just as we do and dreams vivid, lucid, uninhibited, animated scenes. But, unlike us, whose dream characters appear to go "poof" and vanish when we wake up, the dream characters and dream scenes of the Dreamer do not disappear when that dream is over. The Dreamer's dream characters step out of the dream to evolve on their own.

As shocking as this idea may seem, the human body—as well as our stars and planets and other physical things—was created out of thin air from the stuff of a dream. The human body was dreamt.

Authentic understanding about our history will one day involve a deep probe of dreaming.

We came from the mind of a Dreamer. Dreaming is central to the construction of the physical universe. The deity that dreamt this universe began with the original idea—a non-contiguous thought no entity had previously considered.

The Dreamer recognized the potential of an unvalued, overlooked universal material. "Slough-off" is the stuff left behind when an entity moves or engages in activity. Before physicality, slough-off accumulated as if there were universal landfills. Our physical universe was a novel waste-conversion concept that turned into a wonder of creation.

Human beings create their own slough-off in the dead skin cells or tiny strands of hair they leave in rugs and clothes and hallways as they move around their houses. When you vacuum your house, you vacuum up your slough-off. To people who want their house clean, slough-off has no value. It gets vacuumed up and thrown away. However, to a brilliant biologist who appreciated the immense data contained in the DNA of discarded hair and skin cells, the ability to re-create the human project could exist in the same material we just vacuumed away.

Until the creation of the physical universe, no entity had use for slough-off. The Dreamer wondered, could the slough-off of omnipresent beings and other self-aware entities—a material rich in concepts, life sparks, and data—have use in the production of life? Excited by the thought, the Dreamer gathered slough-off from distant places to create a project in a remote section of deep space. Slough-off became the original building material for our universe. When taken into the Dreamer's mind, slough-off could be dreamt and become animated.

In the belief that slough-off had value, a project began. Humanity is simply the most recent stage of this project.

The human body is animal. The intelligence of the body is plant. Our flesh and bone are holographic. When our senses are stimulated, our brains have the ability to create stories. Our stories—the meaning we put on things—form perceptions and identities and other psychological constructs. Our stories result in what we are.

The human body came from slough-off. Slough-off served as the clay for a new sculpture. The artist was a Dreamer. Now, through eons of evolution, humanity is a dreamer too, creating its own sculpture and its own future.

Why does the night sky look as it does? When you look at the stars, you see a construction of galaxies that resemble the Dreamer's mind. The solar systems that comprise the physical real estate of the universe come from the Dreamer's mind. From a mind that can dream, our suns and planets emerged.

Thanks to the Dreamer, there is a grand vision in your future. One day, you will discover a solar system awaits you in a distant location. An entire solar system belongs to you. It has your name on it. From your solar system, with its sun and planets, black holes, worm-holes, and vast space, you are invited to create your own universe before leaving the containment. Should you ask to see it, you have that right. It belongs to you.

The physics of the dream and the physics of atomic structure are very different. Consequently, a third medium was employed to hold the two together—a holo-gram consisting of pixels—you could say "zillions of pix-els"—that shape themselves to thought. The hologram of this world mirrors atomic structure, but more closely fits dream physics.

When you first step out of a dream, you step onto a hologram, one that looks like the earth but is not.

Few people today have ever touched the "real" earth. Those who walk the real earth, for the most part, are traditional people whose ancestors lived for generations in harmony with the earth's seasons and cycles. The Aborigines in Australia—the ones who remain in their traditional world—walk the real earth and are aware of the dream and the Dreamer. Nearly everyone in the modern world walks in the hologram and has never touched the real earth.

The hologram in which we live and play our human games is a magnificently designed illusion of pixels that morph or shape themselves to thought. The thoughts that shape our world are held in consciousness to be projected onto a multi-dimensional screen where we live and experience our holographic games.

We create holographic images out of the thoughts of humanity held in consciousness, where they project onto the earth screen.

The book you are holding, the chair on which you sit, the four walls of your room, the blue sky outside your room—all of it is a holographic medium. The real earth is protected from our thoughts of destruction and illusions of power. When the "bad guys" cut down the rain forest, they cut down trees in the hologram, never touching the real earth.

When I first began to look at the world in this different way, instead of feeling deceived by this holographic environment, my respect for the deity able to create such a reality deepened. I would look at a stone wall, maple tree, an open field, or a great cliff and realize that I was witnessing pixel images, like a digitized collection of dimensional dots that with the application of consciousness could morph into anything—cars, planes, houses, or scenes of nature. A movie projector beaming images onto a screen is a crude but accurate metaphor of the holographic world that surrounds us.

The reason we perceive a tree to be a tree involves agreements in consciousness. While people have differences in perception at the surface level, humanity has agreement at deep levels. Our world is a consensus reality consisting of beliefs and stories held by the thoughts of humanity. Our reality was formed by psychological constructs to which we agree.

An unveiled glimpse into the physics of how our world works stimulates appreciation for the incomprehensible imagination behind it. Physicality has extraordinarily rich detail at the level of construction.

The Dreamer had collaborators in the construction of this universe—entities that assemble realities with thought, employing previously formatted source material. When you construct a house, you are unlikely to manufacture every component from scratch. Sinks, tubs, tiles, and pipes come prefabricated from a factory. Source material that has been formatted with thought is like sinks and tubs. You pick what you want from other realities and put it into your new reality rather than creating every component yourself. Creativity comes in how you assemble your components. The second type of creator is like the contractor who assembles components using previously formatted material.

The material used in creation originates from Source. Everything you see and touch is made of source material. When source material is touched by thought, it is formatted. Source is the generator and warehouse for the untouched, pristine, unformatted material of creation. Source is also the only thing that has no identity and no awareness of itself.

Source has never created anything, even though the material of Source is used everywhere in creation. Self-aware entities are the creators, manifesting by thought.

Occurring naturally from Source in a rare and mysterious event—like a volcanic eruption, hurling pieces of itself beyond its rim—the birth of a self-aware entity is an event that occurs when Source material is pinched off or hurled from Source to land outside, contained. It is not understood why Source does this, but when it does, entities are born—one to fifteen entities in an average birth, although thousands have come on rare occasions from a single cause.

Every natural entity birthed from Source possesses its own unique identification or signature, and its own individuated abilities.

The "first born" in a birth from Source is usually a self-aware, omniscient entity. When self-awareness is not present at birth, a place or containment is created by other entities to hold the separated-out source material. That material is then taken through a process to create self-awareness.

Source is not aware that it exists. If it ever held an identity or awareness of any kind, it would cease to exist. It would lose its nature. Source pinch-offs are different. When Source erupts or burps, a pinch-off of Source appears that is different than Source. Pinch-offs are self-aware. Through evolution, self-aware entities may become aware of themselves in everything.

Our physical universe was created by Source pinch-offs that became self-aware.

Perhaps because they are rare, naturally born entities whose origin is Source create projects where more self-awareness can be "engineered." When an entity-created project is organized and evolution is involved, the new awareness always involves evolution by design. When an engineered awareness is created and realizes its design, it joins the universal family, co-creating side by side with naturally born entities.

Our physical universe is an engineered reality. Human beings are developing an engineered awareness.

Some naturally born entities developed ways to make themselves very, very small and enter the containment from the outside. Inside the containment, they became physical, even though they pre-dated physicality. Not created for physicality, natural entities can be challenged by physicality. On the North and South American continent there are approximately 250,000 naturally born entities holding the hope that they will birth out of the containment at the time of the Great Turning. They understood the risk coming here—that they could be trapped in physicality. For the most part, they are trapped in the illusion that the world of physicality and limitation is real.

Are natural entities better than engineered entities? No, they are not better. Can engineered entities leave the containment at the time of the Great Turning? Yes, they can birth from the containment in the time that is coming, just as natural entities may leave.

In the awareness of deity, no one looks down upon humanity. No one looks up to the first born in creation or any other entity who is older or "more evolved." Differences exist in the universe of entities, but the awareness of deity sees the preciousness of life in all. Unlike humanity, deity sees no hierarchy.

We have a future self that experiences life from the unconditional awareness of deity. In that future time, separation is healed and unity-with-all experienced. In a time that is coming, the understanding of deity will prevail on earth.

Curiosity

In the 1960s, I was a tireless organizer, crisscrossing the country to encourage students in universities and high schools to support civil rights and mobilization against the Vietnam war. To my way of thinking, getting 300,000 people to generate media attention and public opposition to war and racism was good for the country. I had passion for my causes. I wanted the United States government to withdraw from Vietnam. I wanted justice for disenfranchised Americans. I fought for democratic participation in private and public institutions.

My intention was to make the world a better place.

Knowing how to right public wrongs may have seemed more difficult after my 40th birthday, but passion for social change never waned. I searched more earnestly for root causes. Understanding the cause of social ills or suffering, I could join others to alleviate the cause. I never questioned my need to fix the world. How could I? Human suffering was a fact. Social inequality was obvious. Where bad guys dominated governments, good guys were needed to shift the balance of power. My desire to organize for social change evolved, but I never questioned my need to fix problems. Fixing was an internal bedrock.

In the summer of 1992, my bedrock developed its first seismic crack. I was traveling to Brazil to produce a concert that would launch a "campaign for the earth." Heads of state were assembling in Rio de Janeiro for an Earth Summit. My organization had the sponsorship of the United Nations for a globally televised entertainment event designed to invite the world's public to save the earth from human mismanagement.

Everything that could go wrong did. I encountered irreconcilable divisions in my production group. Another production group in Brazil became antagonistic towards our UN relationship and sent negative faxes about us to our sponsors. In the end, my partner and I join the two operations into one group only to have our popular lead band withdraw two weeks before the event when the pregnant wife of the bass player had a miscarriage. The Brazilian television company that granted us our television feed out of Brazil withdrew from the event when the band pulled out.

With every satellite feed out of Brazil committed, concerts in various international cities took place without Brazil's television hook-up. I was blamed for events I felt unable to control, self-sabotaged from places I couldn't see or understand.

My Rio disaster was followed by the collapse of other projects, one after another in a descent I could neither comprehend nor stop. I felt like a stone someone was skipping across a lake. When I touched the surface, there was intense friction. When I got elevation again and movement towards a new project, I was only jumping into the next pool of friction. The distance between my crisis points was shortening; finally, I sank like a stone to the bottom of the lake.

I lost two companies. I lost my family, multiple homes, and investor's money. It seemed to me that hard work and focus on humanitarian objectives no longer made things happen. I started my personal let-go process from an 80-acre estate with ten homes, electronic gates, and private helicopter, and ended in a state of homelessness. On the street, ego humbled, my dream for a better world was checkmated.

It took collapse to discover there was beauty in the condition of emptiness.

Even in bankruptcy, the sun was shining. Magical gifts to make me smile appeared from nowhere. As I let go of my need to control, I found new reason to trust the invisible. Five dollars came my way just as I was thinking how great it would be to have a latte. Magic happened when I had "nothing" at all.

While my personal descent spiraled into economic depression with no income whatsoever, my internal condition blossomed.

I took a "sabbatical" for four years, living in the spectacular depths of the Grand Canyon and playing with children on the mall in Boulder. With time on my hands, I found delight in simple encounters. Curiosity found a home in me. The more I let go, the more joy I felt. I hitchhiked with strangers like it was the 1960s again. My rigid adult self, empowered by decades of "making it happen," no longer sat on my personality seat. I was a student once more, flooded with new information and understanding about this time of humanity.

Many people have created "let-go" journeys in recent years through experiences designed to release controlling personalities and to bring allowance, sacredness, and acceptance into their lives. One way to experience the unconditional mind is to shatter the psychological constructs of the unhealthy, coercive ego.

Of course, should you prefer, you can live in trust of the universe without destroying your entire world.

As a consummate "fixer," I required rolling thunder as my way to understand. I created shock and awe in my own life in order to comprehend that my thoughts of judgment contributed to the "problem" I wanted to fix.

I realize today that my personal let-go adventure was not a solitary one. Many people have abandoned their carefully constructed, fortified compounds, their security blankets, and their agreements with social consciousness in order to let go. Now humanity is right behind them.

Letting go is a planetary event in the time of the Great Turning.

Social consciousness is a "collective mind" that wants to control and force things. Now our collective mind is being pushed away from the earth as if it were a disease or parasite. The urge to fix the world by blaming, demonizing, and cursing others—politicians, bosses, ex-wives, business partners, polluters, terrorists, and everyone with whom we disagree—ties you into that collective mind.

When you create a thought of anger towards another, it registers as a chemical residue in your own body. How does your body feel about your chemistry of judgment? Ask it. When the environmentalist hates the polluter, what does the earth feel about the hate created to "support the earth"? Ask the earth.

My body never understood the judgments I inflicted upon it. The earth feels people's hate and disharmony when people try to "save" it.

Fixers who curse their "enemy" represent an understanding that registers as a wavelength. The wide range of fixers—whether new age believers, environmentalists, anti-war activists, conspiracy patriots, or moral warriors—operate on the same frequency. It is the frequency—not the specific politics or point of view—that is separating out.

I was born a fixer. I earned my post-graduate degree from the University of Fixing. In making the incredible choice to see humanity from all sides—the side that opposes the horror of modern war as well as the side that feels national security requires military opposition to terrorist regimes—I made a decision to disconnect from the bipolar nature of social consciousness.

Non-judgment as a mindset doesn't see itself as better than the collective mindset. The choice to be curious about everything or walk in the shoes of another is a stage of awareness. To the unconditional mind, there is nothing wrong with any stage of awareness. When you are in the mindset of judgment and fixing, respect and curiosity about the bad guy is impossible. When you see the perfection in everyone, as your spirit sees the perfection in you, you connect to a new awareness now entering our world.

In the time of the Great Turning, the intensification of emotional attack or need to curse your adversary creates such psychic meltdown that let-go can be the end result. In the present time, the blame game no longer works well. Anger quickly comes back on you to create meltdown. Should you experience meltdown, there is beauty on the other side.

Out of the beauty of let-go and the ashes of meltdown, curiosity appears.

Curiosity is the awareness that allows you to feel excitement for anyone's point of view. In curiosity, you can walk in anyone's shoes. In the shoes of another, you become intensely curious about whatever you engage. Curiosity never finds anyone to fix.

You can't fix something unless you first see a problem. When you are in a system that wants to repair, that wants to fix and correct and modify, you have to first see a problem in your mind. When you are in the natural universe—the unprotected universe where thought is instantaneously realized—the idea that something needs to be fixed or something is wrong can destroy you. In this physical world with its time/space buffer, you can put off the effect of thought for years. You can hate the President, demonize the polluters, vilify the Americans, denounce the Iranians, or attack your former spouse and not immediately destroy yourself. You have time and space to buffer you from your own thoughts of attack. You can throw out a thought, bring it back, check it out, dissect it, and send it out again. You can then bring it back once more for more examination. Eventually, however, your thoughts appear before you.

If you have the mentality of "I've got to fix or remedy this situation," and you are working with pure thought, you will injure yourself instantly. If you are a fixer of any type in the raw universe, you will first create a problem in order to fix it. That Midas touch becomes a painful experience if you are thinking about problems.

The way to heal something is by not needing to. If a person is a healer and he or she says, "I've got to heal this sick person," the first thought that goes out is that someone is sick. Then the healer has to remove his own attitude of illness before he can work on the attitude of illness with whomever he is trying to heal. If a healer realized that nothing needed to be healed—everyone was in a state of perfection—and someone came who wanted to be healed, then healing would occur by seeing the person in perfection. Such healing does not work as an intellectual concept. It works when there is a deep knowledge that perfection exists, that the person is beautiful and 100-percent perfect in the choices of his or her life. With that knowledge, the thought of perfection goes out and allows the other person's body to build itself up by dropping away its self-directed negativity. The person who holds someone in perfection creates a bridge for that person to walk out of their negativity, should they choose to do so.

The greatest healer who ever lived was the one who saw there was no one to heal.

Many political activists, spiritual people, consciousness workers, social fixers, and humanitarians are challenged by such understandings. Who is not? That deep reasons exist for everything, that perfection is always operating even in a world of pain and suffering, is a difficult concept. The idea that our own thoughts of hate towards the "bad guys" somehow contribute to the problem is rarely considered, especially when our "cause is just."

When you walk in the shoes of another, you understand that every cause has its deep reasons. When you enter the state of curiosity, your defensive armor disappears.

In the time of the Great Turning, you want defensiveness to go.

When you ask someone to draw a picture of a spiritual path, it is often an image of sacrifice built upon concepts of humility. It may also hold colors of anger that flare up at reports that the rain forest is being destroyed. Does anger about rain forest destruction fuel the chainsaws? Does loving the rain forest and its creatures intensely, rather than hating the people cutting down trees, give power in consciousness for the tree-cutters to be educated?

Our historic revolutions were based on anger. The revolution that is coming has nothing to do with anger.

In crossing over from anger to respect, judgment is replaced with preference. You have preferences but are no longer emotionally attached to any outcome. Knowing you create your own reality, the need to blame others for your own creation melts away. The idea that thoughts are completely insignificant is replaced with the understanding that thoughts are primal. Every thought is important, and you take responsibility for every thought you create.

In such understandings, you discover you have the power to move masses and touch minds when that power is channeled with respect by an individual who sees everything in perfection. Such a person heals what an entire world wants to destroy.

The one thing every human being wants to know is that they are okay. When you have even one person walking the earth in total harmony with the understanding that everyone is okay because perfection is working—not as an idealized, Pollyanna attitude but as a deep knowing—such a person creates a reflection or mirror in which others can see they are loved. When an individual walks in the strength of mind to know perfection, they heal and change and cause quantum leaps wherever they appear.

The attitude of controlling in order to get a certain end is that of a fixer. Whenever you are trying to fix something, you hold it in an image of imperfection. You see something wrong. When you maintain the understanding that all things are in perfection, you may not understand a particular situation, but you know at a deep level there is perfection in it.

In the state of perfection, you are shown every step. Your guidance is clear. Creativity floods you. You trust the perfection before you. You dissolve your bonds of defensiveness. Curiosity replaces your need to blame.

Curiosity is an experience of elation that tickles the person you observe.

Life won't engage the person who needs to fix. The separation process now occurring with social consciousness is a protective mechanism for the in-coming reality of life.

Imagine you were born very powerful. Imagine you are a great wizard. Whatever you think happens. So you invent this beautiful world. Your best friend sits next to you and thinks, "Look at that little flaw over there." Now, maybe that little flaw was a special touch you put there, a crystal-clear, pristine lake you were delighted with. Here comes your friend who says, "If only that lake wasn't there, everything would be perfect." Instantly his thought removes your beautiful lake. When six billion people are doing this to each other, it turns into war. You quit creating because whatever you create, the person next to you un-creates.

Out of eons of fixing based on perception, the Great Turning appears. Perception is a world of judgment. Life has no judgment. Life is the awareness of comprehension. Comprehension sees everything as perfect. Perception reasons things like that little lake need fixing.

In the in-coming reality, everyone will give you the respect and space to allow your creation to grow and blossom because life is the in-coming reality.

This is not a condemnation of fixers. The human condition is based on fixers and there is nothing wrong. Evolution will not coerce fixers. In the time of the Great Turning, fixers birth into a world where perception, judgment, and fixing continue. You live in the perception of problems-to-fix as long as you choose.

For those moving out of judgment, curiosity is coming. Curiosity is the excited, non-threatening attention you give to everyone. Curiosity is an attractor of life. Awareness of life gives you life. When life is touched, you create activity that nourishes life. You infuse life into every intention. Like the omnipresent intelligence that wants to know every side, curiosity lets you walk in the shoes of anyone. With no one to heal because nothing is wrong, people are healed. With nothing to fix because life is in perfection, the world around you changes and blossoms into perfection.

Curiosity is the awareness that sees no one wrong. The future of humanity is curiosity.

Fixing is a stage of awareness based on a binary principle—on/off, yes/no, right/wrong, good/bad—also known as perception. Perception produces judgment. The only awareness we have known—our need to blame others for what is wrong—is now separating out.

Evolution is a journey from perception to comprehension. After comprehension comes intelligence. Intelligence is an awareness of your Self in all things simultaneously. Comprehension is the platform that sees nothing wrong and every event in perfection. Perception, on the other hand, sees something wrong and wants to fix it. Comprehension sees nothing wrong and has nothing to fix.

When you are a fixer in perception, you choose the people you give life to and reject those you want to tune out. Your respect for others is turned on and off, using that binary on/off switch that went into your hand when you were issued clearance for travel into this world. Perception is an interrupt system, employing that on/off switch. Life is a continuous flow that has no interrupt. Life emerges when the awareness stage of perception completes and comprehension appears.

Comprehension is the only awareness outside the containment.

An omnipresent entity sees its preciousness in everyone. Life is engaged as sacred. In the natural universe, there is no contrary thought, or behavior that is self-defeating, destructive, or hateful of yourself or others. There is nothing to which you hold back your respect. You engage life unconditionally without judgment. You have your own ideas, and they may differ from others, but a thought of separation never occurs outside the containment.

In the time of the Great Turning, comprehension enters our world, causing the on/off mechanism to separate out. There is no on/off switch in the next stage of evolution. Curiosity is always on. The life switch is always on.

The American dream of life, liberty, and the pursuit of happiness has been a dream not just of Americans but of all humanity—an impossible dream when we lived in perception. In perception, life is interrupted. In perception, life can never be touched. The vision of life never takes root where separation exists. How can it? Life is unconditional. Life judges no one. Judgment and life never exist side by side.

Many people hold the vision of a new humanity. Preparing to understand that vision, they have been facing their demons, learning to let go, releasing beliefs and stories that no longer serve them, and peeling away their judgments like layers of an onion. For years, those who would create a new humanity have built bridges into social consciousness to serve as the pivot point for these years of transition.

Now the human condition is about to swing. It may swing one way or the other and chances are about equal that either way could prevail. The present moment is a crossroads for consciousness, with one direction head-ing into a celebration of humanity and the other into despair.

A direction of despair may cause the human condition to succumb to certain viruses or other events now being seeded into the world. Should hopelessness break out as the dominant choice of consciousness, the economy can be expected to follow in some version of depression. Despair is one direction that humanity may choose as it lives out its blame games and end-stories of the Jihad/Armageddon variety.

The other direction causes an extraordinary uncorking of curiosity to enter the world. Should this direction be chosen, curiosity in millions of people will outshine the best of times as a critical mass aligns with evolution's natural direction towards a new humanity.

Those who seek a new humanity must face their need to fix the world.

Nothing seems to challenge us more than comprehending the fixer concept. The person who feels inspired by the unconditional state in one moment intensely judges the "bad guy" in the next. An environmentalist who hates the polluters may barely comprehend what it means that he or she creates thoughts of hate in consciousness. When those who support a new humanity allow their own consciousness to experience a deep sacredness for all people, including polluters and other "bad guys," it registers in the whole of consciousness.

The new humanity is sparked by those who heal their separation with love for every human being.

You do not need permission to evolve. Should you detach yourself from social consciousness and claim the right to create your own experiences, you will become the author of your life's journey. However, should you tie into the thoughts of humanity, expect to experience the intensification of judgment now occurring in consciousness. If you find yourself wondering, "How did I create this? Why am I so anxious?" you have touched the fear and intensification of anxiety now swelling in consciousness as a new pressure enters our world.

Social consciousness has engaged a state of anxiety like no other time in history. If you have an alliance with consciousness, you may feel the chemistry of anxiety set off in you even when nothing is wrong.

How do you free yourself from the anxiety of others?

Begin your flight of freedom by not condemning others. Judgment and blame pulls you back into consciousness. To disconnect from social consciousness with its condition of contrary, embrace the human condition before taking steps to walk out of it.

The human condition got you here. You and your ancestors came from perception. Everything you ever did and every judgment you ever made contributed to your development. Any part of you that you ever denied is welcomed now. Invite every place in you that fears to come forward. You want to feel your fear, and feel it deeply. Accept your fears as your spirit accepts every part of you.

Does your spirit tap its foot and make endless lists of all your mistakes? It does not. In fact, your spirit sees you made no mistakes at all—none. That is the awareness of comprehension. Comprehension is not based on ignorance, nor is it Pollyanna-ish idealism. It is a stage of awareness that understands there are deep reasons for everything. You could say judgment is misinformed.

Embracing your past, you realize you have nothing to forgive. You were always in perfection.

With nothing wrong, you are ready to embrace your future. Speak your intention for the future with the voice of authority: "Social consciousness is no longer my reality." Know that you have permanently disconnected from all your alliances in thought. Know that you are free from your social harnesses. You create your own reality now. Your need to judge is complete. Seeing yourself in everyone, anywhere you go, you walk in the shoes of others as if they were you—because they are. You might not choose to be the murderer, but you know you could be the murderer. With the gift of omnipresence, wanting to know every side as your way of understanding, you feel the deep reasons in people's lives. Seeing yourself in everyone, you polarize with no one. Understanding that thought has power, you create thoughts of separation with no one.

In the unconditional mind, life pours into you to unlock an unbounded curiosity towards everything you engage.

Who can walk out of the human condition and not condemn anyone? Who can do this? You can do this. Is it possible to end judgment and still function practically in the world? Yes, you can do the "impossible."

As millions of people spoke out against the war in Iraq, and millions of others supported what they believed necessary to protect their world from acts of terror, polarization set in and intensified as each side blamed and cursed the other. As positions hardened, it became difficult to see the humanity on both sides.

Conflict is natural to the time of the Great Turning. Intense conflict comes into the world to create freedom for all sides. When two people are in conflict, both seek freedom. Conflict lets them see what the problem is.

When conflict is compressed, it goes into the genetics of the next generation. Today's conflict has its roots in the DNA and the compressed conflicts of our great-great-grandparents.

What should one do about a world in conflict? People in comprehension know that out of today's conflicts, something more magnificent than anything they could have imagined will emerge.

If you want to make the world a better place, the need to fix the world is your trap. Fixers see something wrong. Fixers have decided something is wrong. When you no longer judge, nothing is wrong. When nothing is wrong and there is no one to fix, the world changes before your eyes.

Can you see that those who choose Armageddon are not wrong? Those who protest war are not wrong. Those who fight wars or make wars are not wrong either. Can you sense that without the capacity for non-judgment, social consciousness will pull you into perception and blame, into the collective mind now separating out?

In the time of the Great Turning, you will make a choice. You will choose to fix the problem, or to create from the awareness of curiosity.

No weatherman is needed to know which way the wind blows, not anymore. Many people know they live in the time of the Great Turning. The invisible signs and stirrings sensed for years are now visible to those with eyes to see. Perhaps the magnitude of the coming change is underestimated, but the significance of this time is understood by millions of people.

For those of you who need evidence that judgment and coercion are intensifying in a new stage of evolution, you have only to watch what happens to people in judgment or people who want to force things. The physics of coercion is intensifying worldwide as it prepares to separate out. The time to pass the torch of evolution has come. Everything new for the in-coming reality has arrived. Everything ending has entered the stage of descent. When a reality comes to conclusion, a universal compression resolves or squeezes out everything that will not be taken forward. Everything that does not serve the new paradigm will see itself completing.

Life has entered the world. In the present time, life, liberty, and the pursuit of happiness can be experienced. If you would soar, you can feel life like a great wind coming under your wings. As consciousness plays out its last act, the going-out of the old reality and the coming-in of a new humanity occur at the same time. You wake in the morning and feel the edges of life entering your world.

The world that is completing has rarely known respect. Examples of respect by a few individuals are available, but humanity as a species has used the physics of coercion, not respect. By physics, I mean the way something operates or works. The physics of coercion is a way of materializing by forcing atomic structure. The human mind is used to force atoms into cohesive, coagulated forms. Respect does not coerce.

If you could see into atoms and understand their physics, you would realize that a car or a house is actually a collection of atoms that have been pushed together by the mind. The things around us have been formed into the objects of our desires. In future times, a person will literally create out of his or her body. It's a strange concept indeed, but nevertheless a car or a house will one day be created by taking a portion of our own sacred being and turning it into the object of our desire, using a form of manifestation common to the natural universe outside the containment. A portion of our own being is morphed or molded into what we want. The bed you sleep on is yourself. The vehicle you drive is your own embodiment. The home you live in is a living piece of your own entity.

As extraordinary as this idea seems, all entities outside the containment create worlds and realities out of their own sacred being. During the transition years, there is a brief opportunity for people to learn how to create in this manner. In human history, shape-shifting has been achieved by some but not many. Shape-shifting is a stage of awareness known to certain tribal ancestors, but it is a rare occurrence in our history. Such creative power requires the conscious understanding that in every moment, everything that belongs to someone is part of someone. By holding that understanding constantly, you learn to create out of your own embodiment through a respect for all things. Those who are birthing out of the containment into the natural universe at the time of the Great Turning may want to learn this ability. Those who do not learn this deep level of respect now will learn it later. In time, everyone choosing to evolve will acquire this form of materialization.

In the present time, the universe supports a deep level of respect. When choosing respect, you embrace life, polarize nothing, judge no one and find cause for curiosity in everything. For you, perception is ending. Comprehension is arriving. Life is before you. All that is required now is that you take charge of your thoughts.

Should you choose to support humanity in the time of the Great Turning, chances are you share an impulse with millions of others seeking comprehension. When you complete the need to blame, demonize, or make others wrong, your activities support the respect necessary to create a new humanity.

For those of you who feel drawn to a new humanity, dream big. Let your dreams become outrageous. Bring new possibilities to a world where options have expired. In your dreams for humanity, see every side uniting. Where you encounter sides, be among all sides. Know that every human being is precious. Feel your excitement for the preciousness that exists in everyone.

When someone is a human being, is that not sufficient reason to give your joy and curiosity to them?

Thinking About Existence

The part of us that thinks it exists is one of the most considered subjects of philosophical discourse. One of the most recognized commentaries on existence came from the classical French philosopher Rene Descartes. Descartes deduced his existence by the observation that he thought. "I think, therefore I am," he wrote. Descartes' axiom continues to hold an honored position in philosophy more than 300 years after his death.

Despite the grand confidence one detects in Descartes' philosophical assertion, I suspect he was not unlike the rest of us, deep in the private cellar of his own mental doubts. Thinking about existence has a way of making us uncertain about it. Thinking seems to fuel doubt about everything, especially existence. "I think, therefore I doubt" may be closer to the real human experience.

Descartes' questioning of existence didn't disappear just because common sense suggested that the act of thinking required a thinker. Long after his reasoned connection between thinking and existence satisfied his inner philosopher, I suspect a question lingered and something in him continued to ponder: Can I count on my existence when I wake in the morning? Is my existence temporary? Will my awareness exist after my death?

The existence that Descartes called "I am" is a human birthright. We claim our birthright when we are ready to end our fixation on doubt. Eternal life is something we choose whenever we end the doubt and guilt and self-condemnation generated by eons of "thinks."

In the course of human evolution, few of us ever claimed our right to exist. Only a few have been able to quiet the question of existence by answering it. Instead of taking life as our birthright and guaranteeing our existence forever, humanity created death, a totally unique concept that exists in no other place but this universe. We replace the ecstatic state of life with the illusion of death by holding tightly to a stage of awareness fixated on "think."

We think. We are aware that we think. Does that mean our awareness is guaranteed? On that question, humanity has doubts.

Is there a stage of awareness where doubt is gone and our existence is eternal? Is there an awareness stage of "forever"? Someone who is forever knows at the core of their existence that they possess life, no matter what else occurs. Where life is possessed, can anything extinguish your life?

Life is the gift you give yourself, not by thinking, but by loving yourself so intensely you love yourself into existence, forever. Evolution is self-selecting. You give yourself the gift of existence when you are ready to love yourself into existence.

Instead of loving ourselves, we feel ashamed, unworthy, and afraid that we have done some horrible, horrible thing. Doubting our magnificence is part of our history. It is one of the gestalts in consciousness. When we realize life is never in doubt, we end our uncertainty and fear leaves our world.

Doubt has been a human oppressor. Doubt is the cause of our "victim" beliefs. Doubt disappears when trust in life returns. Doubt is impossible in the person who has secured life in an awareness of forever.

For those who embrace the forever mode in their awareness, there is a track on which the evolution of awareness runs. In the time of the Great Turning, you can get on that track to move at the speed of thought. During the years of transition, you can engage life so as to propel yourself through millions of years of evolution. Now is the time for those who desire to birth their awareness of "I am" into a permanent existence, using the fast track of evolution. You "forever" yourself when you give yourself the awareness of life. When you chose to make life a gift to yourself, your awareness can never be taken from you.

What is awareness?

Awareness is the ability to engage electrons. The evolution of awareness involves increasing your capacity to engage electrons.

Electrons are intelligent. They go anywhere. What holds them in place is a force—the force of fascination. Electrons become intrigued and fascinated by whatever awareness focuses on them with its inner sight.

To engage electrons and create inner sight, you need two elements. If you want something to have the ability to reason, "I think, therefore I am," two components are taken and bonded together.

One of those components must be a primal element. Although any primal element will do, in the physical universe only one primal element—hydrogen—is available. In the construction of awareness in this universe, you use hydrogen as the primal element.

The other element you require is not found on the periodic table. There is no name for it and no simple way to describe it. You could say it is an element with the ability to engage electrons. Since awareness is the ability to engage electrons, an element must be found that will allow electrons to flow through it.

The starting point for awareness is (1) hydrogen, plus (2) an "electron flow." An electron flow has no awareness and hydrogen has no awareness either. But bonded together, awareness results, if only at the most elemental level. With hydrogen and an electron flow, attention can be created and awareness born. These two elements come together like sperm and egg to create the "primal awareness child." They form an eternal unit that will pursue electrons in its environment. The ability of that awareness to register electrons as they move through this elemental system creates the illusion of attention. Attention is the ability to view electrons.

When electrons are viewed, they behave in whatever way they are viewed. Electrons follow whatever attention they receive. Some physicists suspect correctly that matter is created by viewing electrons.

Electrons can instantaneously clone or duplicate themselves, millions and millions of them at once. The electron was the original design for this holographic universe. When electrons are viewed, the resulting attention creates a visual cortex. When a visual cortex moves upon its attention, that is the beginning of thinking. Thinking leads to interactive or network thinking, which we call intelligence. With intelligence, the evolution of awareness begins.

All entities begin as a visual cortex. Without a visual cortex, there can be no awareness and no way to evolve awareness. As more electrons or attention-getting experiences move through a visual cortex, awareness matures. Visual cortexes don't necessarily mean "seeing with our eyes"—that sensory perception unique to physicality. No entity outside the containment sees the way we do. But all entities have a visual cortex.

From a visual cortex in a primal state of awareness, the evolution of awareness can unfold into an unlimited being.

The blueprint of evolution holds a design that pulls us from a primal level of fixation attention into an awareness of our unlimited existence. In that process, awareness has stages.

The first stage of awareness forms the foundation for "I am." In this initial stage—the stage of fixation—the awareness locks onto electrons. When attention is locked on, electrons only flow in one direction. This early stage of awareness involves a hypnotic trance in which only one pattern of electrons is engaged. Attention is fixed. The electrons form a representation of the fixed perception.

For an awareness to grow, the fixation must be interrupted and released for more electrons to flow into the unit. The universe incorporated a design that would break our obsession or fascination with electrons, employing an interrupt system called ego. Ego was designed to interrupt the fixation of the awareness so that more electrons could be viewed and more electrons could flow into the electron flow unit.

A healthy ego that loves attention is part of our human design. Unhealthy egos are human creations.

In the fixation stage, awareness is limited because the electron flow is limited. As more electrons flow through your awareness, the awareness becomes greater. The more one can avoid fixating attention, the more awareness expands.

Consider the person who is obsessive about wanting something, who becomes fixated on getting it. Fixation limits one's ability to engage the universe to bring in what you want. Fixation limits possibilities to one direction. The evolution of awareness involves a progression from fixation to openness, whereby you learn to let go of your focus and open that fixation so that electrons can flow and possibilities expand.

The brain chatter of thinking is a form of fixation. Awareness is not what you think but what you don't think. To have an expanded awareness of "I am," it is best to stop thinking about existence.

Like peripheral vision, awareness is what you allow in by not looking directly at it. Electrons flow when you don't watch them. That internal dialogue that goes think, think, think—rarely quiet in one's whole life—actually limits possibilities to the object of the thinking. Breaking the focus of the think process, you reorganize electrons. Reorganizing your electrons, you change your reality. That's how miracles are created. As you detach from your "think," electrons reorganize. You pull in more electrons when you are in a state of non-thinking or non-judgment.

Expanding awareness comes down to just two words: let go. It is the process of letting go that engages more and more electrons in the visual cortex.

In the evolution of awareness, the visual cortex is what humanity calls soul or spirit or "I am." The body ages and succumbs to death because of our consensus reality about death. Nevertheless, the genetics of the body are eternal. The awareness of the visual cortex is eternal too. The body's genetics and the awareness unit that occupies the body and lets us think and feel and exist never dies. Awareness is a permanent feature of that visual cortex once the primal element and electron flow are bonded. Your awareness lives through all your stages of evolution.

Most of humanity is in the fixation stage of awareness. In the time of the Great Turning, you can move out of the fixation stage into new stages.

Those choosing to do so are dropping their judgments, opening to guidance, reclaiming their innocence, and engaging more strongly the electron flow. It is the awareness of not looking that pulls in more electrons and moves one along the fast track of awareness.

The shift from one stage of awareness to another occurs when the flow of the engaged electrons become greater than the body can chemically support. At that moment, everything shifts. The need to rebalance body chemistry marks the moment when a new stage of awareness begins.

Many people who have spent years becoming less judgmental and less fixated on making things happen are evolving out of the stage of fixation. There are now enough people on earth engaging more electrons for a critical mass in consciousness to emerge. That critical mass—perhaps fifteen percent of the human race or more at this time—is a new humanity waiting to birth.

In a new humanity, there is a movement away from forcing, fixating, and coercing. Defensiveness begins to drop as openness and curiosity enter the awareness. As more electrons flow through the visual cortex than was possible in the stage of fixation, awareness increases and there is a new source of power. You touch power when you allow electrons to flow. When touching power, you may also feel a tendency towards power trips.

The moral wars gaining intensity in the world are one way to prepare for the right use of power. Expressing themselves as a need to hold judgment about everyone and everything, moral wars allow awareness to learn and evaluate the right use of power that comes with a release of fixation.

In the state of curiosity, you learn the art of let-go. You learn to allow electrons to flow through your visual cortex by not fixating or looking at them. You create minor miracles, although perhaps not consistently. You notice synchronicities created by your own ability to reorganize electrons and shift reality. You have magical moments. Your healing powers begin to emerge.

In the frontal lobe of the brain, every judgment you ever made is stored as memory in the form of chemistry. When your mind is unconditional and you engage the awareness of life, every judgment stored as chemistry is going to be brought to the surface. If you ever judged anything in your entire life, you experience those judgments—coming into you as anxiety or the chemistry of worry. Nothing is wrong. Life clears your mental debris. The chemistry of judgment clears as a natural process. The anxiety will pass as you clear yourself of old judgments.

Engaging more electrons may cause you to believe you are a god. You are a god, but a fearful one. That fear is the chemistry of judgment releasing from the frontal lobe. "God neurosis" is actually a natural experience at this new stage of awareness as every judgment you ever had moves to the forefront. Many people have spent years moving through their judgments and guilt to prepare for this new stage. They prepared so that when it comes, it will not be so intense. You should not condemn yourself should you experience power and then anxiety. Should you find yourself in god neurosis, put yourself in a room alone and give yourself permission to experience yourself as god for an hour. Let someone who knows you provide a reflection as to whether you are getting fixated on that power. Getting through the god neurosis stage is not accelerated when you deny or stuff it.

When the experience of increased electrons is mixed with a controlling personality, you may never let go of the power. When you can't let go at this stage, that fixation retards the chemistry-balancing process. If you get stuck in god neurosis, the body can die.

The only way you can live physically after reaching this open stage of awareness is to reclaim your innocence. You may never leave the god neurosis stage until innocence occurs in you. With innocence, you learn to disengage electrons. Innocence is pure surrender. Instead of doubt, there is a deep trust whereby you allow electrons to fill you. When you put an unhealthy ego on the personality seat, you can never touch innocence. Once power is touched, the brain must let go or the body and mind can no longer mature as designed. Lethargy sets in, and death of the body can follow.

In the stage of innocence, the understanding "I think, therefore I am" comes to completion. There is a loving good-bye to "I think" and a deep embrace of "I am." The brain that thinks stops running certain organs and other functions as it once did. The brain learns to operate invisible aspects of yourself, as the solar plexus region becomes the body's new brain. The think process that once defined an earlier stage of awareness fades into extinction like the dinosaur.

As you touch more and more electrons, innocence is required. Innocence is the fail-safe mechanism to ensure that an awareness that has touched power learns to use power properly. You learn respect. You learn to let go. Where previously you engaged electrons, now you allow your life to be pulled by electrons.

Of the many personalities and identities we have created for our lives, innocence is found in your child, who retained its understanding of innocence through all the years of development. Now that child needs to be found and returned to the personality seat. Where is your child?

You find your child by feeling your preciousness.

As you first wake, when you are half awake and half asleep and the brain is in alpha, let yourself feel your preciousness. Then drop to a deeper frequency and feel (not think) your innocence. Let an unsullied innocence take control of your center of communication. Your mind is natural without ulterior designs. That is your child. That is your innocence.

In the time that is coming, controlling personalities don't need to be kicked out, just reeducated. Teach them to be curious. Teach them to be students. Teach them to watch the magic when the child returns to your life. All the identities that were controlling, judgmental, self-consciousness, unnatural, body-avoiding, and needing to prove themselves no longer occupy your personality seat. They no longer run the show.

With nothing to prove, the personalities necessary to the stage of fixation can now be playful, magical, and passionately in support of the child who is eternally engaged in curiosity about what is next in the great mystery.

The child comes forward as the controllers step back. As the controllers relax, the body relaxes. As the body lets go, it puts you on the fast track of evolution.

In innocence, your body may experience a new love for sensuality. It wants to be touched and nourished. In the stage of innocence, the need to size up every situation for sex and judge every person sexually releases. Innocence creates no pressure on the body to perform sexually.

For those who would guarantee their life, the road to life takes flight on the wings of innocence.

The more you are the child, the greater your awareness. The greater your awareness, the more life you can contain. The more you contain, the more you love yourself. When you intensely love yourself and find nothing wrong with yourself, you give yourself the eternal gift of life. You guarantee your right to forever.

After innocence comes the stage of shape-shifting. In shape-shifting, you can have no judgment at all. Judgments form holes in the biofield attached to your skin.

You need purity of thought to shape-shift. Without purity of thought, there will be self-destruction.

Christ psychosis and god neurosis are healed in the state of innocence. Once you fully engage innocence, you begin to engage all the forces of the universe. I love, therefore I am. I feel precious, therefore I am.

In the time of the Great Turning, the expansion of awareness dramatically accelerates in the person who can enter the state of innocence.

Campaign for the Earth

The primal brain is the primitive, reptilian brain out of which all our instincts come. It handles coordination and physiological functions as well. Where the brain stem joins the second brain—the brain of reasoning and logic—there is a membrane on the brain stem. A tissue pulled tight over the "head" of the brain stem, this membrane resonates like an eardrum. Like any drum, it picks up and registers frequencies and vibrations occurring nearby. As this membrane developed, it registered a rhythm or frequency on which consciousness formed. Buried within the brain, it is able to pick up the rhythm of whatever is strongest around it. It is where intuition comes from. Telepathy occurs here, and your dreams register on that membrane as well.

When a person is in proximity to a particular frequency or wavelength for an extended period of time, the brain stem membrane will pick it up until that wavelength becomes your consciousness. The drum of the brain stem is the place where consciousness began its journey of development.

The body was designed to follow evolution's blueprint. Accessing the frequency that attracts the blueprint occurs when the brainstem membrane picks up a rhythm or cadence emitted by the earth.

The rhythm of the planet is a beta wave. When beta registers on the drumhead of the brain stem, the body accesses the blueprint. It knows what to do, what hormones to release, and how to align with the blueprint's design. When your body is aligned with the rhythm of the earth, the body has the road map for evolution and moves through the stages of evolution held by the original thought.

Should the rhythm of the planet register as a 9 (Hertz), then social consciousness emits a frequency that registers somewhere between 12 to 15. When you pick up a nine on the membrane of the brain stem, you access the blueprint. Most of humanity moved away from the nine long ago, and instead picks up the frequency of consciousness.

The frustrations, irritations and hostility increasing in the world reflect the frequency of consciousness registering on the membrane of the brain stem.

Humanity began modifying its beta wave drumbeat more than 3,000 years ago. Instead of following the blueprint, we follow the thoughts of humanity or social consciousness. Consciousness is directing evolution today, not the blueprint of evolution. As a result, the brain stem is not evolving. We are stuck in the frequency of consciousness, trying to evolve with consciousness rather than the blueprint. When we experience confusion, frustration, anger, or the rut of circular thinking, these are symptoms that result from consciousness trying to evolve the brain stem.

Older cultures—Aborigines, for example—remain in harmony with the planet, but the modern world has mostly lost touch with the earth's rhythm. In the time of the Great Turning, you can move out of the spectrum of consciousness and return to the earth rhythm. You can shift the drumbeat of the brain stem when you reconnect with earth's beta. Should you choose to do so, you experience an entirely new relationship between your body and mind, and between you and the earth.

A portion of the brain called the "third brain" was created to sense and create space. Without it, we would have little comprehension of space. The third brain, located at the top of the skull, enlarges and exaggerates so a person can observe and feel subtleties. The third brain allows for higher vision and thought. It gives us dance and other advanced motor movements. It is a tool for refinement of thought, reasoning, and logic. Taking something and blowing it up into a large picture, we can see it and allow reason to occur.

The third brain registers as alpha on the drum of the brain stem.

Meditation will take you into alpha. Many people, wanting the bliss of alpha, prefer to stay there rather than beta, not understanding perhaps that the brain stem cannot grow when you are in alpha. For the human body, it is the natural beta wave of the planet's rhythm, not the beta of consciousness nor the alpha of the third brain that maintains your alignment with the blueprint. Alpha waves are necessary to develop the third brain. You want to spend time in alpha. But for the body's development at this time, you don't want to spend all your time in alpha.

You came here to take a body. Ask the body what it desires—alpha or beta (not the beta of consciousness but the beta of the natural rhythm of the planet).

How can you access the beta rhythm of the earth and bring the blueprint into the body?

By the expression "sacred power spots," people mean certain places on earth where a refined energy is felt. The natural rhythm of the planet flows from the earth at these spots. Many people don't believe power spots exist anywhere else. They do exist, but they are clogged up by consciousness. People may believe they need to travel to special power spots to access the rhythm of the earth, but they don't. The planet puts out its natural rhythm every 18 inches across the entire surface of the earth. Power spots are located every 18 inches in the form of a triangle everywhere on the globe.

The earth is a rotating orb. The electromagnetism generated by the earth's spin builds up and requires release through its cells or outlets. Without outlets, the orb would melt down. Just as every cell of your body releases the thoughts that you have, the planet also releases out of one of her cells or plates. If you magnified the earth until you could see through it, you would see these plates are in the form of 18-inch triangles. Every orb has a triangular blueprint. The planet radiates its electromagnetic rhythm through these plates to maintain its integrity as an organism, just like people have skin that allows the body to breathe through cells.

The planet respires at locations every 18 inches on the surface of the earth.

You can feel the earth's cadence in your feet at the points of the triangles. The earth's radiation leaks at the triangle points. When you touch one of those points, it may feel warm or even hot or it may create a tingling sensation in your feet.

Power spots are typically places where a culture or some individual has cleared the earth's cells of consciousness, perhaps through ritual or ceremony. In the time of the Great Turning, an abundance of power spots can be re-established everywhere on earth with ritual.

A campaign for the earth—one that would be appreciated by the earth—would turn the entire planet into a power spot. When an individual visualizes the rhythm of the earth coming into a consciousness-clogged triangle point, it clears.

As long as you are not in a fix-it mentality, this is a way to allow the entire planet to clear and express herself. When you encounter a clogged cell, putting your mind in alpha through meditation will not clear it. When you meditate at power spots to experience your alpha wave, you don't experience earth beta. Instead of alpha, bring up the natural rhythm of the planet with your mind, and the entire line you are standing on will clear. Not only the earth, but every person on the earth benefits when you assist the earth in its own desire to clear its cells of social consciousness.

In a campaign for the earth, humanity benefits by getting the drum on the brain stem back to its natural rhythm so we can access the blueprint. The earth benefits by having her expression back.

When you return to the natural rhythm of the earth, the REM state of the dream, bouncing off that drumhead membrane, will also lift you into the enjoyment and body-healing of deep sleep. In addition, your body keeps up with the blueprint as the in-coming energies accelerate in the present time.

Earth power spots and sacred vortices are all about yesterday. The entire planet is a power spot. You can find the natural rhythm wherever you walk. You don't have to retreat to the mountains or oceans or sacred sites. You can access the rhythm of the earth through a city sidewalk. You can find it on the fortieth floor of a high rise.

When you access the earth's rhythm, you allow the planet to express. She, in turn, will allow you to express too. You will have a healthier body and a more peaceful mind. Your body was built for this earth rhythm. Accessing evolution's blueprint through the rhythm of the earth, your body is prepared for the time of the Great Turning.

When the blueprint bounces off the drumhead of the brain stem, the body easily navigates the time of the Great Turning.

If social consciousness is cleared from the earth's plates so that the planet returns to her natural rhythm, earth changes may not need to be intense. The earth is now separating out from the games of humanity. By clearing clogged power spots, you support the earth in her decision to slough off the holograms stuffed onto the earth's surface. When the earth clears, the planet becomes a healthy organism again. It may not need to unleash its "Armageddon viruses." It may moderate the coming ice age. Humanity can assist the earth to complete its clearing of consciousness and replace the human voices of discord when the voice of a new humanity supports the earth.

To access the rhythm of the earth, look to your feet. Find a power spot right where you are. Move your feet around until you find one. Don't avoid the unpleasant spots. Hold the intention that you want the planet to allow you to feel its natural heartbeat. Invite the earth to share her natural rhythm with you. Feel that cadence through the feet. If it doesn't feel good at first, amplify your intention to assist the planet to move into a place where you can feel her natural rhythm through the feet. Put your intention forward. There is no need to put your own coloration on it that it has to feel a certain way. Feel the rhythm of the earth just as it is.

Now, as you walk, feel the rhythm with every step you take. You are in alignment with the earth. You are picking up the rhythm. Your feet are the receptors. They modify your body to reflect the earth's natural rhythm. You walk in harmony with the earth's rhythm. The rhythm is felt and brought into your body.

The human body is designed for the feet to access the rhythm of the earth.

Every nerve ending to every part of your body is found in the feet. The energy comes up, goes through the different meridians and keeps the body healthy and aligned with the blueprint. Your own rhythm is now the rhythm of the planet. Hold this as your intent. If you try to make it happen, you'll stop it. Let it happen naturally. Walk the earth at your normal speed. You don't have to search for it. It comes into you naturally.

Tell yourself that the bottom of those feet cannot pick up any rhythm whatsoever, any place they go, except the rhythm of the planet. Let your feet do the work. There is no step that your feet can take that is not stepping into pure rhythm and bathing your body with it. It is not necessary to image it up. Just put it to the feet. Every step you take is in harmony with the earth.

After a few days, your brain will go on a default setting and make this process automatic. You won't have to think about the rhythm of the earth every time you step.

When you walk in alignment with the planet, the planet expresses through you. When your body knows it takes no step not in alignment with the earth, you have stability and balance. The planet holds the blueprint for you. When you align with the earth's rhythm, your body holds the blueprint. That's how you were designed. You access the blueprint on the membrane of the brain stem. You are in tune with your environment and the environment is in symbiosis with you. You love and support the earth. What could be more beautiful? You love and support your body's desire for the blueprint. What greater gift can you give your body?

In the time of the Great Turning, the earth is your friend.

The Great Turning

In an event that defines the present generation on earth, the Great Turning sets the future for humanity. To those wanting evidence, no scientific response is known. Anyone sensing the potential for global, cataclysmic change in the present generation is going to be pushed into their own natural ability to feel the unknown and sense through veils, employing subtlety or the desire to listen deeply. To the scientific mind, suggestions of this sort are frustrating. Nevertheless, I am reminded of Albert Einstein who created brilliant new science, sitting on his swing or walking down a lonely road, listening to himself inside.

When it comes to gathering data, the human body is a wonder of untapped potential. When it comes to data collection, your human body has no equal.

You have fourteen senses for information gathering. You can employ subtlety—a method for getting smaller and smaller until the hidden can be entered. Through subtlety, clues come to you, perhaps in a small still voice located in the stomach or from internal senses not commonly employed, like radar located in the chest cavity or sonar located in the hair follicles of the ear. Your dreams at night are also significant in the production of your theories about the Great Turning. Your new theory can be tested, even when all you receive is "yes" or "no" from your internal sensing. The process of asking may lead to a model to assist you in interpreting the coming events. When you can sense what is coming, inspiration to embrace the Great Turning follows naturally.

Can anyone know what is coming?

From a state of humility, with the demeanor of a student, an adventure of discovery about this time opens for you. Answers are waiting. You may wish to join other people engaged in similar questioning, where many people in diverse regions contribute their findings and information to a global knowledge network that can be publicly shared. However you do it, you can uncover the time in which you live. You can understand this moment more clearly than anyone who ever lived before you.

Prophecies that forecast great changes coming into the world at the time of the Great Turning span a period of nearly three millennia, the insight of many of the world's respected human beings, standing at the center of wisdom circles in every region and time. The Great Turning was forecast by intuitive people 25 centuries ago in the Yucatan, Hopi Native Americans living in the United States, shamans and Aborigines, medicine men and spiritual clairvoyants, all describing the new millennium as a time of a great collective shift.

Mayans predicted the "end of time" for the years 1987 to 2012. Christians, including many Christian mystics, suggested the time of Armageddon described in Revelations would occur in this current period. The number of people today who believe something "spiritual" and unexpected is about to occur is no longer in the millions but in the hundreds of millions.

Prophecies about the Great Turning tend to fall into two types. One is the "end time" story of the Armageddon variety, that may incorporate a way out of the physical world for certain "saved" people. The return of a Messiah is an historic savior theme. The landing of a city-size spacecraft has been a modern savior story.

The second mindset sees a golden age ushered into the world, the result of a spiritual awakening in large numbers of people.

I mean no disrespect when I characterize deeply-held, sacred beliefs as "story." Story is how the human race evolved. There is nothing wrong with story. Indeed, for most people, the experience of the Great Turning will be the belief they already hold about this time. For example, a belief in Armageddon may draw you into an end-time experience similar to your belief.

Many end-time stories believe the origin of their Armageddon information is God or the Messiah or certain historic prophets. It can be offensive to people holding such beliefs for anyone to suggest the origin of our end-time stories is humanity itself and not deity. I mean no offense to religious beliefs. Should information in this book not fit your beliefs, there is no intention to argue that anyone is wrong.

My purpose is to clarify the role of thought when creating experiences. Out of the beliefs held by human beings, our realities are created. We create ideas about the coming time and our beliefs make it so.

For those seeking information about the Great Turning that is not generated by human beliefs, my suggestion is to take every story and prophecy and set them aside. Open your mind and invite understanding as to what is actually occurring. Is an event beyond the control of humanity taking place, one that is not caused by any human psychological construct? Can we know what is story and what is fact? Can the two be separated? In a physical universe that is a physiological construct, are any facts operating beneath our beliefs and stories?

Yes, facts exist. All our perceptions, beliefs and psychological constructs are derived from about two dozen facts. Cycles of evolution also exist. A new cycle of evolution may be moderated or shaped by human beliefs, but the main event of the Great Turning takes place no matter what we think.

What is a fact?

I define a fact as a reality or creation that is permanent and unchanging. A fact typically evolves over eons and eons as the result of an entity-designed project. Our physical universe is an example of an entity project, one that is still evolving and not yet a fact.

Starting with a concept, an entity project develops. The initial phase of the project may be experimental. When the experiment seems to work, it is then refined, modified, tested, and proven out until it is accepted by everyone as complete. When complete, a reality is then compressed down into a microscopic dot until all that remains is a single, solitary fact. Grand ideas completed and universally accepted are compressed into universal facts. A fact could also be called an "archetype."

Millions of compressed, completed realities exist as archetypes, stored in archives or libraries that serve as resources available to build future entity projects.

The human body may be the most extraordinary archive created to date, although many archives exist. Compressed realities are stored in these archives, like a treasured book might be inventoried in the Library of Congress so it is available for check out. An entity wanting to check out an archetype does not actually check it out and take it to some remote location. Archetypes are checked out for a few moments in order to be cloned. The original archetype or fact is left in the library and the clone version is carried away and put to use. Since a fact is not a living being, an entity must enter the cloned archetype and animate it by becoming it in order for it to be used.

The containment encompassing the physical universe holds 24 archetypes, each of them animated by a different entity that has agreed to accept responsibility for turning on the archetype for the duration of physicality. Twenty-four archetypes form the unchanging foundation or architecture of our universe. Human stories, beliefs, and perceptions may derive from them, but human thoughts are not facts.

Touching an archetype is one measure of awareness. The greater the number of archetypes a human being has touched, the greater that person's awareness. In the history of humanity, the largest number of archetypes anyone has previously touched is 17. At the time of the Great Turning, you can birth out of the containment into the natural universe. To do so, you will have touched at least 13 archetypes.

To illustrate the concept, every human being has touched at least three archetypes that form our environment for basic awareness. These are as follows:

Containment: The physical boundaries of our universe are defined by a containment. If you travel from the earth, and go beyond the seeing eye of the Hubble telescope, you arrive at a place or wall that prevents you from going further. Try this yourself at night. See if you can touch the edge of the universe with your mind. In constructing this engineered space and the boundaries of our physical world, someone went to an archive, checked out the containment archetype and then cloned and animated it. In the shape of a rectangle, the containment formed the initial construction used in the creation of physicality. "Slough-off" gathered from the natural universe outside the containment was the building-block for the experiment of developing awareness in mass and matter. A new concept in evolution, the purpose of this universe was to create a new awareness inside an organic medium. Could awareness develop out of slough-off?

In the initial development of physicality, before the containment was employed, slough-off was gathered and placed in a deep-space location. The slough-off material was held by mind. As slough-off reached ever-larger quantities, it developed a remarkable ability for protocol, that is, it defined itself by choosing to exist in this space but not in that space. Anytime protocol of this sort is demonstrated, it suggests a potential for awareness to evolve one day into an omnipresent being.

As slough-off awareness evolved, it continued to show other remarkable properties including an ability to enter mind. That ability caused concern that it could potentially result in slough-off entering the source of mind. There is only one source of mind in the universe. Because slough-off had thoughts of separation and unworthiness from its beginning—it saw itself abandoned by entities—slough-off awareness became lethal, not only to the mind that contained it, but to every entity in the natural universe.

Why was our physical universe lethal? A thought of separation in the natural, non-physical universe would cause the thought-reactive material that forms the universe to separate. Consequently, physicality was a deep-space experiment that had the potential to end the natural universe. Utilization of the containment archetype became a requirement for the experiment to continue safely until separation could be healed. The containment archetype was designed so that nothing inside could escape and nothing outside could enter. That way, any awareness developed inside the containment would remain inside until sufficiently mature to heal its belief in separation and leave physicality in an awareness that would not threaten the universal family. The containment protected a thought-sensitive universe from lethal thoughts expected to occur during an immature stage of awareness.

Cleavage: A second archetype brought into the containment involved the principle of cleavage. That which is whole is divided in order to create something new. When something new occurs using cleavage, the separation must then be healed as the new creation comes back to wholeness. Separation in this universe is rooted in the archetype of cleavage. The birth of a child from its mother is cleavage at work. Our stories of Adam and Eve are derivatives of the archetype of cleavage. The splitting of the atom is another cleavage principle. An interrupt system (on/off) or polarity of any type—good and evil, right and wrong, yes and no—are all derived from the cleavage archetype, from which a binary reality can develop, supporting awareness to evolve through perception.

Refraction: A third archetype used in the development of physical life is the refractory archetype. A reflection principle, it allows a hologram like this one to reflect awareness. Operating like a great mirror everywhere in the containment, it creates a method for an awareness to see itself, should any awareness develop. When you think something about yourself, you get a reflection to validate your thought. That is refraction working.

With these three archetypes—containment, cleavage and refraction—an awareness has the capacity to see itself. How we see ourselves is how we evolve and come to exist. An awareness creates itself by what it thinks about itself. What we believe ourselves to be is what we become. An extraordinary concept, evolution is self-selecting.

Through various stages of development, the human project emerged. There are 23 chromosomes in the human body. Chromosome 23 holds all of the data about the history of humanity. Twenty-two chromosomes, some of them having 300 million years each in linear time to develop, hold the rich history of our entire biological origin. You can ask to see chromosome 13 or chromosome 5. See what images come up for you from your deep, non-human past. You can ask to see what your feet look like in chromosome 9.

Developmental steps leading to the human project might be described as follows: (1) entity slough-off established protocol; (2) slough-off was placed in the mind of a dreaming entity; (3) slough-off was dreamt, giving it animation; (4) the dreamt or animated dream characters separated from the dream in a cleavage principle; (5) separated from the dreamer's mind, the new, animated awareness was able to generate "thinks" as the result of sensory stimulation. Should an awareness generate a think about itself or someone else, the awareness instantly saw a reflection of its thought that mirrored back its own self-awareness; (6) once an awareness was able to identify with its own reflection and then with reflections from others, perceptions about itself started to grow.

A containment filled with reflection is an evolutionary strategy for an awareness to evolve through its own psychological constructs.

While no one ever determined what our human perceptions would be, certain human stories that recur generation after generation, such as the Trinity (Father, Son, and Holy Spirit), were derived from this initial triad of universal archetypes. These three archetypes form a center, not just for Christianity, but many human belief systems.

The facts that comprise this world are buried beneath our layers of stories. Stories we have heard. Facts are mostly waiting to be discovered.

The Great Turning is a cycle of evolution described by the blueprint, one that is not controlled by psychological constructs. You can step into a new staging of evolution or not--that is your choice--but a reality shift in a great cycle of evolution is not a creation of the human mind.

The Great Turning is a time when a veiled evolutionary stage completes. Every stage uses the earth for a particular development. The human project is a stage of evolution. Evolutionary projects march onto the earth and then off again, one after another, over eons. Each has an allotted time to affect its design. When that time is over, the completed reality gives way to a new staging.

The allotted time for a particular staging is governed by a "time viral." Time is not a constant but an engineered thing, the result of a viral or knowledge module that sets the mechanism of time for a particular staging. The time viral for this world sits in a shell at the center of the atom and winds down over a 35,000- to 38,000-year period. We are currently 38,000 years into the present staging when "completion of time" may occur at any time. When a time viral expires, a new time viral replaces it, marking the juncture of the Great Turning. Holding information for the incoming reality, our new time viral is now replacing our historic time viral.

Sensitive people may already feel that time is changing. They sense that time is becoming more fluid and able to expand and contract based on one's own thought, and they are correct. Physicists will soon realize that certain understandings empirically developed about atomic structure are also changing. The change in atoms is due to the expiration of the historic time viral, causing a decaying of atomic structure until the new time viral fully replaces the core of the atom. Other changes, such as volatile weather and the degree of the earth's wobble, lead up to even larger changes in the arrangement of land, atmospheric composition, time-space fluidity, gravity and other phenomenon that mark the end of a staging.

We could use the metaphor of a theatre performance to describe the Great Turning. The curtain closes on one act, the stage setting is taken down, and the next set put in place. When the curtain opens again, the scenery and the actors' costumes may be different. The play continues, but the look of the actors and appearance of the stage can change. You could say the theatre of physicality is a play with a million acts, each running a duration that is set by a new time viral. As an actor, you are encouraged to write your own play as the performance unfolds. As a character's story develops sufficiently such that its awareness can be carried over into the next act, it evolves, from one act to the next, through the entire million-act play. At the end of the play, 98 percent or more of the characters will have developed and matured into entities with the awareness of comprehension and able to birth into a place outside the theatre walls.

Will you experience a new stage of evolution in this lifetime? You may without ever knowing any change occurred. If you choose to keep your world as it is and not proceed towards the next evolutionary staging, no significant act change seems to occur. If you are not moving into the next act of evolution, you wake up one day, apparently in the "same world" you just left, never knowing anything happened. Your children may be gone or dear friends may have disappeared, but your memory of them is erased. Nothing is different to you except perhaps some haunting memory of those you have lost. Your life seems normal and you continue to evolve in the world you "always knew."

The Great Turning is veiled. Should you choose to bring your unconscious evolutionary choice to a conscious level, more information about the crossroads of evolution may come to you through the veils. For most people, however, the Great Turning will stay hidden and no particular evolutionary moment will dramatically appear. If you choose to birth out of the containment at the time of the Great Turning, however, you will experience the most dramatic event in your existence.

We are familiar with various cycles—the cycles of earthly seasons, moon cycles, and solar cycles. A staging cycle may be routine to the intelligence that created this engineered space, but it is not known to humanity. A large cycle of evolution—the Great Turning—was veiled throughout history, even to those able to sense something extraordinary about to happen in the present time. Now, for this generation, the veils open when you ask to know.

The year 2000, as marked on the human calendar, began at midnight, December 31, 1999, serving as a human metaphor for the Great Turning. A new year, a new decade, a new century, and a new age on one night everywhere in the world, the majority of humanity believed this calendar change was significant. Christ was coming. Armageddon was coming. Comets were coming. UFOs were coming. Whatever one's story about the millennium—and they included end-time beliefs side by side beliefs that the millennial anniversary was just another calendar change—the global party became the most focused event in consciousness ever to occur up to that time.

The new millennium was a psychological construct—the page turning on an inaccurate calendar—not a natural cycle like the Great Turning.

The immediate significance of December 31, 1999, in consciousness was that it set up disappointment in the thoughts of humanity. On the night of the millennium, sacred beliefs about end times were not experienced in consciousness. While the night itself was an extraordinary expression of humanity, the despair and disappointment that set in afterwards is still held by consciousness. The war on terrorism, calls for Jihad intensifying in the Middle East, the outbreak of deadly new viruses, and other global events are expressions of this lingering end-time scenario that failed to happen at the millennium but still seeks expression and completion.

Since human vision beyond the year 2000 is almost non-existent, there is little to catch the psychological crash felt in many people after the millennium. Millions of people choosing to step into the next staging may feel drawn to weave mythic vision into a global safety net to catch the hangover crash after the millennium. As disappointment fuels a growing intensity in consciousness, it invites alternative visions of global family and a new humanity

Creating options for no-option regions is not about "fixing," but creating new possibilities for people facing a giant identity crisis at this time. Authentic vision can be a safety net under this world for a time when consciousness fails and humanity believes its story-lines have run out. As despair sets in, consciousness will look for a place to go. Exhausted by blame games and intense side-taking, people may see your vision of unity and non-judgment as a place to go.

With passion to catch humanity in its post-millennial letdown and inspire others to consider the unlimited options possible in this world, you are the midwife for the birth of a new humanity.

If you long for sacredness to find expression on earth, now is the time to prepare your vision of sacred society and weave your net to catch and break the coming psychological fall. The time has come when your dreams for a new humanity can be embraced by others.

There are veils in this world. The veils are by design. What is hidden is veiled. Our origin is veiled. Evolutionary stages are veiled. Our life purpose is veiled. What happens when we die is veiled. We have beliefs about such matters but little or no evidence about what is veiled.

In the time of the Great Turning, the veils are thinning and you can discover authentic information hidden to every previous generation.

Consider the veils that surround "death." A recent American television program called "The Dead Zone" suggests new public interest in the subject. In a popular interview format with a television host able to link someone in the dead zone to a living family member out of the television audience—a wife or child or aunt of the dead person—a televised exchange is offered nightly in which a dead person answers questions that only the person in the audience can know to be true. Audience members often cry in joy over answers from the dead zone.

People have beliefs about death and life after death. Many people have faith in an eternal life that exists after passing from the physical world. But for most of humanity, veils define the dead zone and we freely admit we do not know what happens when we die.

Are the veils that surround the dead zone thinning?

Consider these clues. Ask inside about them. See what you uncover by contacting the part of yourself that knows all about the dead zone. Let these clues form a pathway to walk through your own veils about death.

In the history of the universe, has anyone died so far? If people are living after "death," where are they? What is the address of the dead zone? What is it like to go there? What is the relation between your thoughts about heaven and what actually occurs when you show up in heaven? With questions like these, give yourself permission to receive authentic information from the parts of yourself that know. You are the first generation able to do so—to understand what actually happens when you die. An opportunity to access previously veiled information has opened to you.

When you die, your awareness releases from the spinal column and travels out of your mouth (not the crown of your head), where you step into a familiar containment vehicle—your dead zone body—an electrical body that allows you to travel to the dead zone address. The precise location of the dead zone is through the atmosphere to its outer layer, the stratosphere.

The experience of the dead zone is shaped by your own beliefs about death, no different than when you are living. In the dead zone, however, your thoughts are able to manifest quicker. If you are falling, falling, falling in the dead zone, you soon discover that all you have to do to stop falling is stop falling in your mind. Everything responds to your thought. You can create whatever you want and experience whatever you missed in the physical world. You can be married and have children in the dead zone. Then if you want, you can leave the children and your marriage, and no one is injured and nothing is wrong. Ascended masters holding a view of their elevation in humanity created a place in the dead zone above everyone else. At first, they lived above the stratosphere. Over time, ascended masters got so elevated in their mind that they left the atmosphere altogether and set up operations on the moon. A "silly idea," but ask to know if this is true. Is the physical location of our ascended masters the moon?

Let's say you arrive in the dead zone with a deep belief about heaven. That belief has created a place called "heaven" waiting for you. There is a place that looks just like your belief in heaven in the dead zone. Another extraordinary creation in the dead zone is the golden chambers of the Pharaohs, created in Egyptian times, but still vibrant and inviting today to anyone who knows they are a pharaoh when they die. You create your own experiences in the dead zone, just as you have in this world. When you write a will, you do it for others. When you write a personal cosmology for death, you do it for yourself.

People who loved themselves while living, generally keep their self-awareness intact when visiting the dead zone. People with unworthiness or self-hate in their Self image are going to have their defeating, contrary beliefs erased over time. If you hold beliefs contrary to your own evolutionary interest, they are going to be erased when you die. After the erasure process, what remains is your beauty and existence, which cycles back into the world as a newborn child. Some people take up permanent residence in the dead zone but most of humanity returns to the world again and again.

Before you were born, you wrote your own death cosmology.

The men and women in the Twin Towers on September 11 made choices about life or death right up to the last minute. They were choosing a death experience to affect the world—an event they believed could support a uniting of humanity in the time of the Great Turning. Like them, we also choose our death experience. We choose our birth experience as well.

At birth, does the child choose the parents or do the parents choose the child? The child chooses the parents, every time.

With these unsubstantiated assertions, I mean only to encourage you to consider your new situation: You can ask questions and receive authentic information about previously veiled subjects in the time of the Great Turning. If it doesn't happen for you the first time, stay open and steady with the process, giving yourself permission to receive answers through the veils.

In making contact with the dead zone, I personally choose not to connect with the dead or ask for information from the dead zone. Instead I have a "sentinel" who is an expert on the dead zone. Anyone dead, wanting to contact me, contacts my sentinel (my own psychological construct.) If my sentinel receives information considered important to my development, the information is passed on or I can meet someone dead in my dream. Otherwise, the dead zone is not part of my own developmental process at this time. I want to be free of the dead and of social consciousness. Neither serves my purpose in the time of the Great Turning.

Some information that comes to you through the veil may be unlike any previous human understanding. Beliefs underlying humanity's moral wars may be challenged by your new information. Not intended to make others wrong, the new information you discover nevertheless will find its way into consciousness where it may question beliefs held in consciousness. For example, consider the woman who chooses to abort her unborn child and faces condemnation from others that she is a murderer. It is true that life exists in the unborn fetus, just as life exists in freshly-cut flowers. But who made the choice to abort the life—the pregnant mother or the unborn child? In asking that question, you may discover that the child makes that decision, every time. The child also chooses a mother who has her own deep reasons to support the unborn child's decision to pick up certain developments in the womb but not continue into a physical life. There are deep reasons for an entity to come from the dead zone into a womb and then return to the dead zone before a physical birth. The deep reasons previously veiled can be sensed through the veils as well.

You choose your birth. You choose your death. Now you are about to choose your next staging of evolution.

In the time of the Great Turning, something rare occurs—a moment in creation when the natural universe clicks off and then on again. In this moment, a human being can "birth" out of the containment. Should you ask for that birth ticket, you can rocket out of the containment, under incomprehensible force, your conscious mind intact (maybe), your "data" reduced down to fit through an atom-size pin-hole in the containment and land outside, in the raw universe. The next time a birth of this type will occur in linear time is estimated at 30,000,000 years, with another million zeros behind that—longer than the age of the present universe.

As a stage of evolution is completing on earth, a universal birth moment is occurring as well, opening a portal for a human being to birth out of the containment. In the time of the Great Turning, you can choose an "impossible" dream.

It is expected that some people will choose the "birth option" and leave the containment. For those staying in physicality, there are various other options. What we all share in common is that everyone makes a choice and picks one of the options.

When a cycle of evolution completes, evolution pushes you hard to get off the fence and make a decision. In the time of the Great Turning, we witness new pressures on the mind. Everyone makes a choice—any choice is fine, but choice is a requirement. The new pressure in the world is the result of a pushing on people's psyche to make a choice.

Choices are made at a deep level. Most people have already decided on their next staging. If you are reading this book, chances are you are a person who wants to bring your choice to a conscious level. That is appropriate, but doesn't make you better than the person who decides at an unconscious level.

This information comes to support your conscious choice in the time of the Great Turning.

This information also arrives in the form of very challenging ideas. You may want to run from this information, or you may want to know more. You may want to hear from a small, still voice inside able to say yes or no to this information. Whatever comes up for you, your response is appropriate. There is no need to doubt what you feel. You cannot make a mistake in the time of the Great Turning.

For you who desire to bring your options to the conscious level, there are choices to consider.

Most people are choosing to keep their reality just as it is. Taking a survey of social consciousness close to the issue date of this book, about 60 percent of humanity chooses to follow consciousness and not the blueprint. At the time of the Great Turning, they will wake up in a new holographic world in a seamless nighttime movement in which nothing seems to have changed.

How is this possible?

Some people sensitive to "invisible worlds" speak of dimensions. I use the term "parallel realities." In the space between you and this book are numerous parallel realities on frequencies over a certain band. When a radio is tuned to a particular frequency, it accesses the station assigned to that broadcast band. The human anatomy has an analogous tuning mechanism located in the pineal gland. You have a standard frequency that holds you in this physical world. If you could change your station with the switch of a dial, you would experience another reality within the exact space you presently occupy. In fact, you have numerous Selves living in parallel realities at this moment. Parents of autistic children should know their child may operate in a parallel reality while still in this one. (When you think they don't hear you, they do.) In the Great Turning, people are able to turn their dial and birth onto another band, stepping into a holographic reality similar to this world but not the same. Parallel realities represent a benign solution for those who want to follow consciousness rather than the blueprint during the change that is coming.

In the time of the Great Turning, you can step into "World One," a parallel reality, and never realize anything has changed whatsoever. Many people choosing to stay in this present world will simply walk into a parallel world at the time of the Great Turning without affecting their grip on reality.

The blueprint of evolution, however, marches forward in an awareness change from perception to comprehension. In the choice to embrace comprehension, you enter "World Three," a non-interrupt reality where life is held sacred and the flow of life continuous. There is no on-off switch in World Three. Your curiosity is continuously on. The blame game completes, and passion, excitement, and non-judgment take hold. Respect is the law of your new world. You embrace life as the universe takes you from one magnificent event to the next in a continuous progression of perfection.

At the present time, about 15 percent of humanity chooses to "graduate" into World Three, the coming stage of awareness described by the blueprint. Should you create new options on earth in the years of transition, that number may enlarge as people see and embrace your examples of a new humanity.

Everyone else will go to a holographic "World Two," a gentler place where judgment and on/off perceptions continue but without the intense negativity.

The three worlds that are coming appear simultaneously with a "universal birth" event. In addition to the three worlds described above, you have a fourth option: the choice to birth out of the containment into the raw, unprotected universe in the time of the Great Turning.

If you choose to leave the containment, you will be the first to do so. No awareness inside the containment has ever left the containment. If you sense this could be your purpose at a deep level, more information will come to you. You want to know what awaits you. You want to know how to prepare. Information can be accessed at night by holding the intention to receive what you need to know for an extraordinary journey. You have time to prepare.

Since no one seems able to predict the exact moment of the Great Turning, you are able to extend your time on earth, long into the future if necessary. If you are leaving the containment, you have a "longevity clause" available to you should you choose it. To activate your longevity clause, you simply choose to do so. You realize you have things to do. Between age 65 and 70, your body stops aging if you break your connection with social consciousness and its belief in death. Exercising your longevity clause, death has no hold on you. When you know you can stay physical until the "birth moment" arrives, you have sponsors who will assist you to make it so.

You can also birth out of the containment from the dead zone.

While this discussion may not be understood until the birth moment occurs, there may be curiosity in this subject when people disappear. In addition to this little book, words written in personal journals may also be discovered. To those who discover these journals, it will seem extraordinary how much the "birth option" was understood by those choosing to birth out of the containment. Journals will show that many people knew in advance what was coming, including the horrific gravity force they would experience in the first few seconds and the ecstatic state that would follow as the massive data of physicality, reduced to the size of an atom, hurled through the universe with consciousness relaxed and watching, landing outside the containment.

Any human being deeply desiring to leave the containment at the time of the Great Turning can do so.

If you love yourself and make your best effort to embrace the unconditional mind, you will have a team of sponsors who will assist you with whatever you need for this rocket journey out of the containment. Should you leave physicality, you will still be "contained" in the raw universe for some time until your "rough edges" of awareness get refined.

Leaving the containment now, you may be the first to exhibit some of the new hybrid species described by the blueprint—consisting of Self, Creator, and Source, emerging into the raw universe as an awareness like no other.

The Great Turning is more than a routine theater change. It is more than one act completing and a new act beginning. It is also a birth moment never previously known, at least not in the physical universe.

Whatever option is chosen at the time of the Great Turning, you are about to birth your Self—whatever you have come to believe you are—into a new world of existence.

In the time of the Great Turning, you choose consciously or make choices from a deep level. The way you cross the road is in perfection. If you feel it unnecessary to choose a direction, that is appropriate. Those who embrace the internal sacred experience of respect will find in that decision the natural pull of evolution toward World Three. Those who hold to the judgment and perception of the present world will birth into a new holographic world similar to this one.

When a stage of evolution completes, your mind and body clear. If you have demons and monsters in your memory, they will complete, perhaps by standing in front of you. Ex-wives and ex-husbands may show up in dreams as the lovers they once were. Old relationships from 20 years ago may appear from nowhere. In the time of the Great Turning, the compression forces every thought you have had to come to conclusion. Humanity is experiencing that compression now. In addition, consciousness begins its descent. The physics of coercion that previously prevailed in our world enters retrograde. Beliefs and behaviors rooted in separation or judgment intensify in order to complete. Making things happen with your mind is no longer supported energetically. Those who are moving forward in the progression of evolution should remember that respect—not coercion—is the foundation of the world that awaits you.

To protect your Self from your own thoughts, time buffers are put into an engineered space to assure that an evolving awareness won't have a thought of unworthiness and instantly extinguish its existence. If you were suddenly placed in the natural universe outside the containment and you didn't love yourself, you could be suddenly gone. If you are choosing to birth out of the containment, you want to heal your separation in the years of transition. Thoughts of separation can be lethal out there as they cause the universe to separate. In a seamless reality, based on the physics of "thought-done" or instant manifestation, any thought of separation is a poor idea.

That does not mean there are no individuated entities in the natural universe. Intelligence exits within different entities with different abilities. But entities in the natural universe experience their wholeness.

They know their divinity within and without. They may have different opinions, and those opinions may be strongly held, but the thought of separation would never occur in an unlimited entity. Life experiences involving any thought of separation never occur in the natural universe. When separation or cleavage principles are involved in the creation of new life forms, they are contained until the separation is healed. Before then, they are toxic to anything in the natural universe.

Symptoms of separation-thinking are everywhere in our world: poverty, war, victimization, unworthiness, fearful minds, contrary beliefs, and attack-and-defend behavior. The stories we create are responses to our belief in separation, generating the experiences of our lives. Through stages of evolution, we progress out of separation. The time of the Great Turning is a moment of evolution when you may continue the awareness of separation or move into a new awareness stage. With no right or wrong and no condemnation for whatever one's choice, you stay in the present system of social consciousness or move into non-judgment and comprehension—the choice that assures the energetic support of the universe will come to you from its primal depths. Whatever choice you make, evolution's blueprint continues to operate for you, beckoning you towards your magnificence and the grand vision of Divine Human.

A New Humanity

Humanitarian philosophies and social visions call to the civilized world in proclamations and manifestos from every age. Equality for all, freedom from tyranny, non-violent movements—our calls to humanity have launched democratic change, inspired revolutions against oppression, and galvanized people to lead more compassionate, gentler lives.

Among the visions that solidified into national cultures or working systems of government, the awareness of non-judgment has never appeared. Teachings of unconditional love from world religions encouraged millions of people to reflect on the concept, but only a handful of "saints," representing the smallest segment of humanity, seemed able to sustain the profound experience of the unconditional mind.

Throughout history, judgment has been the dominant human condition.

As challenging as it is to practice non-judgment for five minutes—fifteen minutes may seem impossible— the Great Turning is a stage of evolution holding non-judgment as its deep purpose. Evolution calls to humanity from a long progression of forgotten ancestors. Unconditional awareness will reshape the world, with or without humanity. Non-judgment is at our door, knocking.

A revolution of nature, "divine human" is an experience held by the genes. Passion is eternally generated by a new DNA. In the time of the Great Turning, no religion needs to declare that love shall be an article of faith. No political creed has to issue a constitution requiring respect. Divine human enters the world as a biological event for those who choose it.

Body chemistry does not support a permanent state of joy or passion, although you can image such feelings in. Appreciation and respect in your thoughts produce the body chemistry of joy for a few hours, but it quickly dissipates. You can change your chemistry with thoughts of self-love when you eat, but the experience must be continuously repeated to sustain the chemistry produced by joyous eating. You can open endorphin and opiate receptor sites temporarily with thoughts of wonder. Certain recreational drugs or passionate sex may also offer temporary experiences, but putting the chemistry of joy on a permanent default setting is not yet possible.

In the time of the Great Turning, the choice to love unconditionally creates a new life hormone and new additions to the DNA. Three new rungs on the DNA are set to appear, and when they do, a permanent new body chemistry results, able to support the divine human experience of joy, passion, and life.

No biologist ever told us about a biological revolution. No tradition or science ever prepared us for such a concept. Nevertheless, evolution is at a crossroads, one fork leading to a continuation of the present world and the other towards divine human. The concept of a human biological change may be difficult to imagine, but when the evidence profoundly touches your own life, magnetization towards divine human will seem natural.

Generations of people claimed they were affected by the pull of the full moon or the ionic charge of a thunderstorm. Scientists know that large solar flares on the sun can disable an earth satellite located millions of miles away from the sun. Now, a previously unknown energy—a broad-spectrum life viral—is advancing towards the earth. For years, certain people traveled out to meet and touch this wall of energy with their minds as it steadily proceeded towards us. Some wrote books about their experiences. They described "stellar rains" pouring onto the earth or complained about an intensification of electricity in their nervous system. A few had fevers when they were not sick. Anecdotal stories are not evidence for this unlikely thesis, but in the experiences of these people, we find early indications that people have been able to sense this anomaly now entering the world.

The event forecast years ago by sensitive individuals is occurring now. As a result, desire may grow in humanity for authentic understanding about a new pressure on the mind and body. Life in the body feels like an electrical pressure. It may cause an unfamiliar anxiety or intensify within the body. Emotions result, as body chemistry previously caused by judgment is released, triggered by the life force touching you. Contact with life is like using "mental floss"—it removes anxiety residue so that your body chemistry can rebalance. In the process, it may trigger nervousness, flare-ups of anger or even psychotic episodes. Life cleans out mental debris. Debris is anything that is not life. To touch life is a grand experience. Once you touch it, however, anything within you that is not life will begin to burn and clear away.

Life has entered our world, inflating the containment that holds the physical universe and causing pressure, just like a balloon blown up to its maximum capacity. Its arrival brings a compression that causes incomplete thoughts to conclude and mental debris to end in a fiery consumption.

Combustion chambers within our own atoms are activated by the compression, creating mood swings. One moment, we are anxious and feel a strange pressure in our mind, only to enjoy a new clarity of mind in the next. We get help from the universe to clear away the mental garbage we couldn't remove ourselves. It is a process in which mental negativity may intensify into bizarre behavior—the result of new pressures on the psyche generated by the compression.

There are plants and herbs to assist you if the nervous system is challenged by the overstimulation of life in your body. The central nervous system may be dilating or expanding in order to handle the new frequencies. When encountering such pressures in the nervous system, you can make a nerve tea consisting of valerian root, passion flower, and cramp bark. Valerian root works as a natural sedative for the nervous system. Passion flower assists the nerve endings to open where there is a hardening or sheathing. Passion flower can soften those nerve endings. Cramp bark, sometimes used to dilate the bronchial airways, can also create dilation in the nervous system. When slightly dilated, the nervous system can manage life's electricity until it gets used to the new frequency.

Make your life nerve tea with four parts valerian root, three parts passion flower and two parts cramp bark.

By "life," I do not mean what is commonly understood by that word. Life is not the chemical simulation of life used in the production of emotions. Life is not our psychological constructs or perceptions of life. Nor is it the judgments of others that help us define our personalities and identities. Life is not the mental chatter of the brain that goes "think-think." What we generally call life is an animation that simulates life. Life, however, is something else.

Life is a "material" produced by a source in the natural universe. It is a volatile, high octane, unconditional material. To access life in the human body, you need an awareness to match it. Consequently, a judging, conditional mind will never touch life. You need an unconditional mind to access life. When you make a judgment of any kind, you cut your circuitry with life. In the time of the Great Turning, life enters the brain and comes down the nervous system to create a new biology when the mind occupying the body is free of conditions.

Since the purpose of this world is to create life, there is a season of evolution when everything that is not life separates out. Life is what remains when life passes through a world. Anything that is not life separates out to be preserved and continued in a holographic world.

As people wonder why society is unraveling, or how to interpret turbulent changes or bizarre dreams, they may seek answers in politics, sociology, psychology, economics, conspiracy theories, or history. One may discover symptoms of our time in such places, but not the underlying cause. The underlying cause is evolution. Evolution, in a series of interrelated forces working in symbiosis, is clearing and preparing the human race for life.

When people touch life, many have an epiphany experience. Organized religions may consequently experience a new fervor as people pour into their folds with new intensity. The years of transition may witness great surges in the historic religions. With these surges may come a new season of moral wars.

Where a religious framework provides for little or no tolerance for disbelievers, you can expect high levels of intolerance toward people who are considered outside the faith. People you thought you knew will suddenly become "born again" and turn very opinionated. One cannot condemn them for believing they have touched God. This is their framework for the extraordinary experience of encountering life.

Although the born-again may feel compelled to jump into religious crusades upon the initial encounter with life, that feeling may not last long. Six months after touching life, the born-again person's life may be falling apart. Anything that is not in innocence will compress and combust. Social consciousness can be expected to go through several major swings as a result of life's advance through this universe. "I touched God" will be at one pole. "Why has God abandoned me?" may be at the other.

Emotions are chemical. Feelings are electrical. Life carried into the body through the nervous system is electrical. Life registers as electricity in the body. When it first occurs in you, it may operate just below the threshold of pain. It stimulates the nervous system. The best way to navigate is to relax. You may be in sensory overload. You may experience an overstimulation of the body. But life will not destroy you. It will clear you of what is no longer useful. However, the more active the brain, the more the pain or anxiety may intensify. When you relax the brain, there should be little or no pain.

Cultures based on a natural format will not have much difficulty with the electromagnetic pulse of life. People close to nature, who live in places where losing a job or abandoning a schedule are not traumatic—traditional people and cultures in India, Peru, or Africa, for example—will be fine with the incoming life force. North America, Europe, Japan, and other regions where civilization has developed social structures with rigid controls and a strong mental focus may feel hardest hit and the most challenged when people cannot maintain mental focus.

In the years of transition, governments and institutions may not cope very well. Then for no apparent reason, organizations may start to work again. These are times of intensification in consciousness followed by times of release and expansion. On the other side of the crystalline wall of life, reforms appear. If you try to fix things during a time of pressure, you may be drawn in yourself. Allow the process to run its course. The time for rebuilding follows compression and meltdown. If you are going to be a fixer during a compression time, you will experience compression yourself.

Clearing in the time of the Great Turning is a natural process. A life clearing is like an outbreak of the flu—it must run its course. Give people their space to go through whatever they need to go through. When you do that, you will be a pillar for the new institutions and lifestyles on the other side of the compression.

It is a time when people may pull on your heartstrings. It is also a time when you are served by understanding that nothing is wrong. Witness the clearing. If you go into judgment based on some idea of compassion, you may be pulled out of your own center. If you stay in the awareness of perfection, you will have smooth sailing through the wall of life.

Put your child on the personality seat. Your child knows how to take you through the arrival of life. On the other side of life's clearing, a new humanity awaits you.

Life will not be organized, impeded, manipulated, or controlled by humanity. Instead, life brings humanity to the riverbank. In the time of the Great Turning, every person chooses to cross over or remain on the shore. Evolution does not coerce and there is no right or wrong in any choice. Those with dreams of a new humanity will feel a longing to cross over. Those who work tirelessly for a vision of respect can let the force of the future take them. The coming human revolution cannot be affected by governments, armies, power groups, Armageddon, Jihad, or any other worldly event or belief unless you are tightly bound to such beliefs through your own alliances in thought.

Nothing in social consciousness can deny your right to life. If you disconnect from social consciousness, you can touch the future of divine human now.

What is social consciousness? How do you disconnect from it?

Social consciousness is the result of the thoughts of humanity held by a chemical medium. The medium has weight and size. When a person has a thought or "creates a think," the body's skin emits an airborne hormone or pheromone. Every thought creates this type of physical manifestation. Some people refer to their lingering thoughts as "thought forms." More precisely, a lingering thought is a chemical pheromone with a shelf-life of 40 years, emitting a brilliant radiation through a decaying mechanism that burns and expires over a 40-year period. It is not a living being, but it exhibits a form of intelligence. It floats from the body that created it into the atmosphere where it gathers with other thoughts and organizes with what is similar. Every thought of humanity, held by a pheromone in the atmosphere, adds another building block to social consciousness.

Thought pheromones organize themselves with similar lingering thoughts. Clusters of thought shape our world.

When all human beings agree about something at a deep level, thoughts of agreement organize themselves into a "consensus reality," producing common global experiences on earth. Are scientific "laws" psychological constructs or physical laws? The understanding to that question is found in the discovery that the world in which we live is a psychological construct.

When large numbers of people hold a belief—the Christian belief, the Muslim belief, the new age belief, or any other belief held by large numbers—the resulting collection of pheromones creates a gestalt, to which those who wish to support that alliance in thought connect.

If you are a Christian, you probably connect to the Christian gestalt that has organized itself in the atmosphere. When you are in an alliance with consciousness in any manner, you make a connection using airborne hormones created by your own body. These hormones attach to the crown of your head, and then physically travel to and connect with your chosen pheromone gestalt, or thought alliance, located in the atmosphere.

Can one's connection to social consciousness affect your experience of life?

If you were a Christian living in a "new age town," you might have occasion to meet new age people. If you found yourself experiencing a certain fascination with a tarot deck, or fell in love with a new girlfriend who practiced astrology, alarms would go off in the Christian gestalt to which you connect. It can discharge an electrical signal that comes down your pheromone circuitry through the crown of the head, where it enters your body to discharge chemistry that makes you experience doubt or fear. It can also generate a "brain story" that causes you to ask yourself, "What am I doing? I have lost my clarity. I have abandoned my faith." I am not suggesting anything wrong with any faith. I am saying that once an alliance in thought is made, it takes on an existence of its own in a default setting that continues to operate until you disconnect from it.

How can you know which thoughts are your own and which are the thoughts of others coming in from consciousness? If you choose not to be pulled in by the beliefs held in consciousness, what alliances—if any—should you support and what should you release?

Disconnection from social consciousness is a consideration in the time of the Great Turning.

One reason for such a consideration is that social consciousness currently holds fear and panic unlike any time in history. As a result of an intense new pressure in consciousness, atomic-size concentrations form in the atmosphere—I call them "panic nodules" of a kind never seen before.

Social consciousness is a great collection of chemical pheromones created by thought. If you observed the "thinking output" of Tokyo, New York City, Mexico City, or any other large urban area, it would appear in the sky like a mushroom cloud, the stem of the mushroom appearing directly over the city and the head of the mushroom exploding outward beyond the city in the shape of a mushroom cap, not unlike the mushroom cloud we see from an atom bomb explosion. The mushroom cloud of consciousness, however, explodes constantly, over and over. Your body is able to take pictures of that mushroom cloud, so its image is known to you.

Since the social trauma of September 11, 2001, consciousness has begun creating tiny mushroom clouds within its larger mushroom form. Consciousness is emitting physical drops of "particulate" that have sufficient size, weight, and tensile strength to break off from the larger mushroom and survive the descent as they hurl into the physical world at 60 to 300 miles per hour. An extraordinary development—one never expected by anyone—the entry of particulate causes people who have connections with consciousness to attract this speeding matter into their body. It can strike the spinal column, elbow, forehead, biofield, anywhere on the body, leaving the physical manifestation of an intense fear concentrate.

Should that happen to you, one of these atom-size "angerettes" can cause you to feel considerable anxiety for no apparent reason. Should you have the sensitivity to feel a particulate upon impact, it feels wet and you feel "slimed."

If you are looking to find the mechanism of action that translates human thought into human experience, consider first your own thoughts (conscious and unconscious) and then consider the thoughts of others—social consciousness to which you connect.

The thoughts of humanity held in consciousness manifest on earth. Physiological constructs created by millions of people generate our worldly experiences. When you connect to consciousness, you are going to be affected and pulled into the fear now intensifying in consciousness. Consciousness feels threatened as life enters the world. When you connect to consciousness, you may experience that intensity of fear in your body.

You create your own reality, without regard to what anyone is thinking, when you disconnect from consciousness.

In a popular science fiction movie, a character played by Keanu Reeves struggles to accept the idea that his day-to-day world is not natural but an elaborate engineered space—a Matrix—in which its human inhabitants never know what is real and what is not. In the world of the Matrix, one's personal appearance is a residual self-image, and sensory perceptions are simulated by electrical signals sent to the brain. A neural simulated dream world, the Matrix is a complex engineered reality designed to keep humanity under control. In the movie, Keanu Reeves' character is invited to learn the truth about the Matrix. He is offered a blue pill that assures he will wake up in his illusionary bed where nothing has changed and where he can continue to believe whatever he wants. Or he can take a red pill that will free his body from its neurological social harness and let him see the elaborate design of the Matrix as well as the extraordinary depth to which "the rabbit hole goes." He takes the red pill and sees the truth. Nevertheless, even with his new sight, he cannot initially accept what he sees. The red pill threatens not only the psychological construct he has about himself, but the illusion of his entire reality.

In *The Matrix*, science fiction and the physics of our own world touch together in extraordinary ways, suggesting that authentic, previously veiled information about our world may be entering consciousness at this time. In the movie, evil machines are the architects of human experience. That part is fiction. The way the "real world" works is similar to the Matrix, but the thoughts of humanity, operating through the medium of consciousness, are the architects of our collective experiences.

Our engineered world is a psychological construct created by humanity. "Goody-two-shoes," for example, is a belief held in consciousness about how good people should operate in society—a belief system contrary to human passion. "Victim" is another belief held in consciousness that creates perpetual evidence that human beings should trust no one. In the present time, fear and anxiety are the dominant thoughts in consciousness.

Whatever is held in consciousness happens on earth. At least that has been our experience until now. Leaving consciousness, you can change the "law" of our historic reality.

You are the first generation able to "take the red pill" and uncover the truth of your world. You can discover the hidden role of consciousness in shaping your experiences. You can know how the mechanism of consciousness operates. You can also decide what power to give it.

The thoughts of humanity affect our weather patterns. They define the human condition. When you are aligned with consciousness, your thoughts and moods are affected by other thoughts. Beliefs you share with humanity cause thoughts to enter you from your thought affinities.

Choosing to experience a new humanity, must you free yourself from the thoughts of judgment intensely held by others?

When you feel the understanding to that question, you open a door to a world of your own making, unbounded by the social harness of consciousness—free at last, free at last—to leave the condition of contrary and cross the "great water."

You are not a victim in this world unless you choose to be. When you experience self-sabotage or victimization and you don't know why, it is because you and your ancestors put in place that circuitry to social consciousness. While you have free will, your circuitry remains in place with social consciousness, allowing the beliefs you share with others to shape your experiences until you walk out of those connections in thought. Just say no to consciousness. Otherwise, you tie into consciousness in its time of global intensification and descent.

Let's say you believe "if one thing doesn't get me, something else will." You are aware that most people share your "realistic beliefs." In fact, the collective mindset of "victim" is held by more than 70 percent of humanity. Your victim belief, shared by billions of others, is certain to give you the evidence that proves your belief is true. You think someone will break into your car. At some future time, your belief brings about evidence that you were right—your stereo is stolen.

When large numbers of people believe there are shadowy powers behind our government, pulling the strings on people's lives, there will be evidence to "prove" it. The thoughts of millions of people with whom we align in consciousness produce the experiences in our lives. Our reality is created this way, the result of beliefs and physiological constructs held in consciousness to which we choose to connect.

Understanding the primacy of thought and realizing the many thought alliances we have with others, how do we disconnect from consciousness?

You are hard-wired into the thoughts of others. You have certain agreements with consciousness you may choose to retain. Despite the hurdles to your freedom from consciousness, nothing can stop you from making the choice to create your own reality. Freedom from social consciousness is your right. You can disconnect from consciousness with your mind at any time, and join with others to create your own reality. You can also create your own world without regard to anyone else.

When you disconnect from consciousness, no one can stop you from creating whatever experiences you think. Your mind is that strong now.

You could say that consciousness is the set of rules by which human beings agree to play and evolve in this holographic world. Within the complex grids of consciousness, there exist gestalts and belief systems held by humanity. Taken together, they shape our experiences when we align with them. In the time of the Great Turning, you can walk out of this historic condition to create a new humanity.

There is nothing wrong with the present human condition. Understanding there is nothing wrong, a new humanity has no need to fix consciousness. We make no argument and offer no defense with respect to the experiences that result from it. Consciousness with its condition of contrary and need to blame others for its own creation is no longer our reality, that's all.

In the decision to create experiences free of consciousness, you align with the life force entering the world.

A living gestalt has been seeded into consciousness. Consciousness is not living, but the new living gestalt is. Should you connect to the life gestalt while disconnecting from social consciousness, you discover a brilliant strategy for navigating the coming time in celebration rather than fear.

Passion is also entering your world. A discovery gene exists in every human being. Repressed or turned off in most generations, it went on briefly in the Renaissance, and briefly again in the 1960s. Social consciousness never favored the discovery gene when it was on. Instead, social consciousness offered up domestic harnesses for those who were curious or had passion for life. As a result, the discovery gene has been mostly recessive.

As life enters the world, it causes a new frequency to step up at such an exponential rate that the discovery gene is going on again, triggering epiphany experiences and passion. With the discovery gene on, passion returns and people love their life in ways they never imagined possible.

As life turns on the discovery gene, a natural state of the body emerges, able to operate from both chemical and electrical mechanisms. Passion is more than the chemistry created by the orgasmic state of a heightened sexuality. Electrical passion is more ecstatic than any chemistry.

If I were to choose one prison to unlock in this world, I would say, find the keys to free your electrical passion. Unbridled from the social harness of consciousness, the ability to soar with passion frees everything else—joy, excitement, abundance, life, curiosity, creativity, and innocence. Passion is the experience of freedom itself. In passion, you are present. Passion operates only when you are timeless.

To produce electrical passion, you activate combustion chambers in the body. Combustion is necessary to ignite electrical passion. Desire is a cornerstone in the process. Fascination (focus and curiosity) is an important, additional building block. Silence creates the wick for your passion to burn. (Silence is an ecstatic state itself.) Taken together, using desire as your fuel and fascination as your cause, your passion ignites your wick from which you can move mountains. Passion is so close to being a source that life actually issues from it.

To step out of social consciousness and become the author of your own life, taking responsibility for everything you create, align with your passion instead of social consciousness.

Touch your passion by putting it into words. Excite your passion with your voice. Hold back nothing as you speak. Why is the voice the great place to start when producing electrical passion? A combustion chamber for electrical passion exists in the lungs and throat, in the form of a triangle. The base is formed by the two breasts and the pinnacle is the throat. Speak from the combustion chamber of your two lungs, using your throat as a wick to draw your sound up and out. Your lungs are a combustion chamber for passion. Speak from your lungs. Feel your combustion in the throat ignite as you speak. When combustion is working, the voice should resonate and feel rich. Speak about something you love. Feel and experience how your words resonate through your entire body. State the reason you came into this world. Say who you are. Realize your voice can build things and end things.

In your natural evolution, you unlock your expression of passion.

When you go in and find your passion, you deepen your voice without increasing the volume. It is beautiful and rich to hear your voice when it comes from your passion. Expressing from the combustion chamber of the lungs, your intention can turn words into law. Your word was designed to be law when you hold the awareness of unconditional respect and know you are a lawgiver.

The universe functions with you when you are in passion.

In the creation of passion, that combustion process also activates the stomach, where your source of life is located. Passion is a switch to turn on your source of life. In the ways of passion, unlock the source of life lying dormant in your stomach.

In the blueprint of evolution, you hold a design to become a new species consisting of source, creator, and self. You are the only self-aware entity in creation able to generate within yourself your own source of life. Until now, source and creator have been two separate species. Omnipresent beings outside the physical universe cannot source life. No one on earth has ever sourced life either. In the time of the Great Turning, however, this extraordinary design feature of the human body can activate. If you become a source of pristine life, you will be the first entity to do so.

According to the blueprint, you are a self-aware entity having an unrealized source. Your passion activates your source when you invite it to be part of your life.

Speak to your unborn child with your passion. Speak to your body with passion. Speak to humanity with passion. Ecstatic states are caused by your voice in passion. Your passionate voice will allow your body to pull all its resources together. Bring passion into every cell with your voice as you intensify the fire of the combustion chamber. Find the power that is your passion.

Passion is a state of being. In the time of the Great Turning, you can make passion your state of being.

How can you intensify passion? You intensify passion when you image in with your mind a counter-clockwise vortex, spinning in the palm of both hands, drawing passion to you like a source. As the two palm vortexes spin, feel your passion strengthen as the vortex of passion intensifies in each hand. Experience the passion running up and down both arms. To increase the passion further, put another vortex at the crown of your head, spinning and enlarging the experience of passion at the crown. Now spin a new vortex in your heart region. Feel your passion growing in the heart. Start a vortex in the stomach area. Take time to experience the increasing passion with each new vortex you create. After the stomach, go to your lower back and start a passion vortex there. Allow the passion growing at the tip of your tailbone to gently, gently (without force) rise up the spinal column, slowly to the throat and then up to the crown of the head until your passion overflows, spilling over like a summer rain, covering your face and chest and legs and entire body with your downpour of passion. Let passion bathe you.

State in your full, deep passionate voice: "I am passion." Feel the vibration in your body that is your passion. With passion overflowing from the crown of your head, engage the world with your passion.

Knowing your passion, the future of divine human is touched in the years of transition. In a time when the blame game intensifies in order to complete, passion is a new game entering our world.

For the organization wanting to create teamwork, the business owner seeking the success of profits, the family wanting love, or the Prime Minister wanting to serve and inspire humanity—for any individual, group or nation in the time of the Great Turning—the vision of non-judgment with passion is the bright doorway to success. Making others wrong—whether originating from the fear-based management style of the once successful CEO, or the television talk show host certain that disrespect improves audience ratings—you follow a strategy to end harmony and effectiveness.

The blame game that once worked in the past no longer does. Today's blame game creates emotional backlash, severe psychic pressure, relationship breakdowns, intensifying stress, and lessons in humility to a degree never previously known.

Why are institutions not coping very well?

The physics of coercion is ending. Curiosity, passion, and unconditional respect are appearing. Although the philosophy of non-judgment never took root in previous societies, for this generation, non-judgment stands with unconditional respect as the only strategy able to create family or functionality in business, government, or service organizations.

Where managers seek harmonious relationships with employees, they may want to replace judgment with a new skill—the talent to walk in another person's shoes, whether that person is a client, a vendor, a shareholder, a secretary, a CEO, or anyone deserving respect.

If you are a human being, you are worthy of respect. When disrespect prevails in an organization—the result of thoughts that hold the intent to hurt another, whether spoken or unspoken—the organization polarizes and turns dysfunctional. In the time of the Great Turning, blaming others as the way to hold people together won't work very well.

Those who seek evidence for this perspective may want to observe organizations, families, churches, partnerships and nations in the present time.

Where passion for life and respect for all appear, a new humanity will reshape our fields of knowledge and systems of exchange:

Education: Education today serves as a handmaiden for socialization. In a new humanity, education throws open its arms to curiosity. Rich valleys and deep contours appear in the brain of the curious. The future of education is rich valleys and deep contours.

Commerce: Lack is an interruption of universal abundance. When you gain respect for the life of others, the realm of lack departs. When life is embraced as sacred, the harvest of abundance returns. A new humanity in sacred commerce can never lack.

Politics: Although differing by degrees, democracy and dictatorship share a common precept: their politics is a viral whose purpose is control. When people blame others for their life circumstances, they give their power over. When a person knows his chains were all forged by thought, he or she becomes the antigen to the political viral. Creating your own reality, you re-script the political form.

Technology: For those who love technology, align your inventions with nature and infuse life into your products as they enter the world. The most important component in any technology roll-out is the intention the technology holds from those who created it.

Health: The future of medicine lies in an understanding that the body is both intelligent and thought-reactive. Loving yourself, you heal. In the body's own intelligence lies an ancient knowledge about health and healing.

Laws and Conventions: When all laws and conventions are replaced by one law—the law of respect—and comprehension of the law finds its place in the heart of humanity, the requirement for law takes leave. All that remains is respect.

You live in a time when a new humanity can emerge—unconditional, deeply curious, childlike, ever passionate, feeling its beauty, sacredness, deliciousness, and electrical output in a progression of perfection that is continuously heightened. Releasing yourself from the social harness of consciousness, you realize passion is the root of your Self. In that realization, a new humanity rises naturally out of yourself.

No one can paint a complete picture of what is about to happen, because humanity adds its brushstrokes and storylines to the changing of a paradigm. Although the birth of existence is before you and the rising sea of life is lapping at your feet, it is your choice that sets the future course.

In the choice to respect, the promise of a new humanity is assured.

These are the days you can walk in rhythm with the earth. These are the days your passion for life turns on your discovery gene. These are the days when intense curiosity and passion become your vessel to cross the great water.

The future of this planet is life. For those who claim life in the present time, the dream of humanity appears.

You love who you are. You love that you are outrageous. You laugh at yourself, delighting in tiny things that cause you to laugh again. You love your ability to walk in everyone's shoes. Accepting responsibility for everything that happens in your life, even when you don't know why, you understand experiences come from your thoughts. Your understanding causes you to feel more curious about what you create. It becomes easy to take responsibility for everything you create when you know curiosity.

When something isn't just what you wanted, you say, "Whatever just happened is going to be more magnificent than anything I could have imagined." How can you say that? You say that because it is a law of your reality. In setting laws for your world, you know the ultimate outcome of whatever you create is going to be grand and extraordinary.

Free of the blame intensifying elsewhere, you open your world to the joy, passion and creative power of the unconditional mind.

Long before our physical universe, intelligent entities created with thought. They knew of this deep-space
experiment. They knew of its extraordinary origin and
design. Should they look upon this world and see a quar-
reling, fearful humanity, they would still express awe
and respect. Should they hold a single wish for humanity in the time of the Great Turning, it would be that we
could know the treasure that we are.

To omnipresent, intelligent, unconditional entities,
you are more than wonderful. You are the prodigal child
coming home.

There is an ancient wisdom that celebrates your existence. In the time of the Great Turning, you can learn
the profound cause for your celebration. What a universal intelligence sees in you, you are about to discover
for yourself.

In previous ages, the origin of humanity was hidden,
its extraordinary purpose veiled. Now the veils are lift-
ing. Can you know your origin? Can you know your purpose? In your choice to embrace your own sacred promise,
the Great Turning births your awareness into a discovery of who you are. Your moment arrives. You are wel-
come to exist. You may step into forever. After all, you
are the grand idea. The triumph of evolution is you.

Index

The Author

Rennie Davis was the coordinator of the largest U.S. antiwar and civil rights coalition in the 1960s and remains one of the recognized spokesmen for his generation, featured on numerous television documentaries and media forums, from  the *Legends* series produced by CBS to *Larry King Live,* Barbara Walters, Phil Donahue, VH1, CNN and other network programs. He organized the 1960s most dramatic events, including the 1968 protests at the Democratic Convention in Chicago. For his part in one of the largest media events in history, he was indicted and became one of the Chicago 7, America's most celebrated political trial. The Chicago 7 subsequently became the leadership of a nationwide student strike in the spring of 1970. In addition, Rennie Davis organized the May Day protests, resulting in the largest arrests in U.S. history when a Washington, D.C., stadium was converted into a temporary prison.

When he first spoke out against the Vietnam War in the mid-1960s, few Americans agreed with him. By the end of the decade, the majority opinion embraced his call to end the war in Vietnam and Cambodia. After the Paris peace accords were signed in 1973, he challenged his own political agenda during a speaking tour reported by all U.S. media networks and much of the foreign press. He announced he was leaving the coalition of organizations that had inspired a protest generation to pursue a different view of the future. In 1973, he stated that evolution would create the defining juncture for humanity in the new century.

In the 1980s, he was consultant to the largest U.S. syndication of equipment leasing and real estate and created comprehensive business strategies for numerous CEOs and senior executives of Fortune 500 companies. At that time, he also began a global search for highly gifted inventors holding breakthrough technologies. He assisted start-up companies in capital development and took them public. In addition, he worked with directors and senior management of diverse Fortune 500 companies in executive search, leadership training, financial planning, employee benefit design and executive outplacement.

He is the founder and chairman of the Foundation for Humanity creating new social and technology options for the 21st century. He is also the founder of the Humanity Fund and Ventures for Humanity, technology development companies providing organizational resources for the commercialization of break-through technologies. His leadership in the socially responsible investment industry was recently profiled in the *Dow Jones Investment Advisor.*

All author proceeds from this book are donated to a nonprofit corporation, Gnosis in the Turning of the Ages.

For additional information about The Great Turning or to contact the author:

www.thegreatturning.org